W9-DIS-060

The Romantics

England in a Revolutionary Age

E. P. THOMPSON

THE NEW PRESS · NEW YORK

LIBRARY OF CONGRESS CATALOG CARD NUMBER 97-66267
ISBN 1-56584-360-6

Published in the United States by The New Press, New York
Distributed by W.W. Norton & Company, Inc., New York

The New Press was established in 1990 as a not-for-profit alternative
to the large, commercial publishing houses currently dominating the book
publishing industry. The New Press operates in the public interest rather
than for private gain, and is committed to publishing, in innovative ways,
works of educational, cultural, and community value that might not
normally be commercially viable.

Production management by Kim Waymer
Printed in the United States of America

9 8 7 6 5 4 3 2 1

FOREWORD

This collection of studies of romantic literature in the 1790s presents a part of what was to have been a far wider study of the subject.

Edward Thompson published a major work of scholarship about once every ten years. In the 1950s he produced *William Morris*, a study of the designer-poet and of the political beliefs and actions which informed his work. A decade later *The Making of the English Working Class* examined the actions and beliefs of popular radical political movements in the early industrial period and the working environment in which they occurred. In the '70s *Whigs and Hunters* showed how a single political Act could illuminate aspects of the social and intellectual life of a wide spectrum of the population from dissident tenants of encroaching Whig landowners to forms of Jacobitism which touched some literary and aristocratic circles. In these books as in all his writing Edward was aware of a great variety of forms of literary expression not as 'illustrative' of the movements he was studying, but as an essential part of them.

There were two further subjects on which he had intended to write major studies, one the customary popular culture of eighteenth century England, the other a study of the English romantic movement of the 1790s. When he realised that time was getting short, he drew together his published and

1

unpublished essays on the first of these subjects and published them as *Customs in Common* in 1991. He died before he could do even this for the second, and to him even more important, subject. Throughout the whole of his working life, Edward had been gathering material and publishing on aspects of the romantic literature of the seventeen nineties. As he described it:

> ...the moment when the received culture was challenged [when] all conventions were called into question, and the great humanist aspirations were abroad, but when sharp experience had shown that the periods of the philosophes were inadequate – it is exactly within this conflict that the great romantic impulse came to maturity.

A great part of the chapter on William Blake was published separately as *Witness Against the Beast* in 1993. What is presented here is the nearest we can get to completing the study. Some of the material was given in the Northcliffe Lectures delivered at the University of London in 1983, but the scripts of these have not survived. The material from some of them has been used here in the essays, published for the most part in not very accessible places, or reviews of the work of other scholars and of the large number of re-publications which have appeared in the last two decades. One lecture no part of which appears here is one to which he attached a great deal of importance on the subject of the rights of women in the thought of the 1790s. Part of this was published in another place as described in the short afterword on p. 223, the rest is unrecoverable.

The book is introduced by a lecture given in 1968 in which he offered for a non-specialist audience, some of the ideas which informed his history and his study of the lives and the writings of the English Romantic poets.

The essays look mainly at the work of Wordsworth,

Coleridge and John Thelwall, at some of the intellectual influences on them, including Godwin and Rousseau, and at the political and intellectual context in which they worked. The ideas he discusses are not just those presented on the page by philosophers and theoreticians but also those embodied in the social fabric – paternalism, authoritarianism and the respect for tradition and custom. The effect of the French Revolution and of the Terror are to be seen in the actions of the state and of the power groups in society as well as in the works of the intellectuals who had initially welcomed the rising.

***

The place of publication of the original articles is given in the footnotes to each chapter. The footnotes vary in detail according to the requirements of the original publishers.

Dorothy Thompson
Worchester 1997

EDUCATION AND EXPERIENCE

It is commonly argued – perhaps more so a few years ago than it is now – that liberal adult education offers a relationship between the teacher and the taught which is in certain respects educationally unique.

All education which is worth the name involves the relationship of mutuality, a dialectic: and no worthwhile educationalist conceives of his material as a class of inert recipients of instruction. But, in liberal adult education, no tutor is likely to last out a session – and no class is likely to stay the course with him – if he is under the misapprehension that the role of the class is passive. What is different about the adult student is the experience which he brings to the relationship. This experience modifies, sometimes subtly and sometimes more radically, the entire educational process: it influences teaching methods, the selection and maturation of tutors, the syllabus: it may even disclose weak places or vacancies in received academic disciplines and lead on to the elaboration of new areas of study.

My own discipline, social history, provides abundant examples of this. Many outstanding social historians of this century – R. H. Tawney, G. D. H. Cole, H. L. Beales, Professor Asa Briggs- have been noted for their close ties with the adult educational movements. Areas of study long neglected – and, in some places, still neglected – in university

4

history schools were explored over several decades in university tutorial classes: and today one may still see new offshoots of social history – in local history, in industrial archaeology, in the history of industrial relations, and in that area of contemporary cultural study pioneered in this country by Richard Hoggart – the initiatives for which have often come 'from below', from the adult class and the adult tutor, and not from the academic schools.

I shall return to these points, briefly, at the end of this lecture. My purpose now is to inquire into the larger historical and cultural context within which this notion of 'experience' can be placed.

Raymond Williams has written recently of a crisis central to changing English culture in the nineteenth century:

> appearing in one form as the problem of the relation between 'educated' and 'customary' experience and language, in another form as the difficult relation between intense feeling and intellectual consciousness. [1]

His comment arises from a discussion of Hardy: and, of course, *Jude the Obscure* is a classical study of exactly this crisis. But it seems to me that the crisis cannot be fully understood unless we go back a good deal further than this: and at least to the first disclosure of this crisis in late eighteenth-century romanticism.

If we stand at any point in Europe in the mid-eighteenth century we can observe an educated or polite culture virtually encapsulated from the culture of the common people. 'Persons of rank tend to keep their cold distance from the common man, as if they fear to lose something by such intimacy.' The words are given to the sorrowful young Werther by Goethe in 1774: and they remind us not only of the great social space between gentry and people, but also of the stirring self-consciousness about this space in the Europe of Rousseau. 'The simple folk here already know me,' writes Werther again, 'and seem to be fond of me, especially the children. At first when I made efforts to join them and ask questions about this and that, a few thought I was making fun of them and were quite rude.' 'I know,' he continues, 'that we human beings were not created equal and cannot be': but the very insistence betrays a doubt – a doubt which was to be enforced two years later by the American Declaration of Independence, and which within a further fifteen years was to tear European culture not into two but into several parts.

We must, however, take note of an irony – which is that, the greater the social space, the more room there was in it for illusions to flourish. In the vast social distances of nineteenth century Russia the man of goodwill called out to the peasantry and received back the echo of his own goodwill. In Russia the fictional image of a Holy Peasantry haunted the populist writers – was tested by Tolstoy – flickered still in 1917. It is to be found in the populist and nationalist writers of Eastern Europe until recent times, and it appears to flourish still in the celebration of *négritude* in Africa. We should remember that an affront to the purity of Kathleen Na Houlihan could, less than fifty years ago, cause a riot in a Dublin theatre.

The examples serve to point a contrast. No myth of this intensity can be found in the English educated culture of the eighteenth century. How far back must we go, in English literature, to find a holy peasant? He is there, certainly, in Langland and in Chaucer's Plowman. He hovers still in Shakespeare, less as the agent of effective value than as a reminiscence from an antique age brought to bear in criticisms of the present, like the 'good old man' Adam. By the seventeenth century he is effectively banished into a decorative figure in the pastoral eclogue: and there he remained, with tedious tenacity, through much of the eighteenth century. But the holy peasant was never one of the fertilizing myths of English culture in this century.

We might come at the reason from many directions. Great as was the social space between the gentry and the labouring poor, it was not so great as in eighteenth century France – certainly not so great as in nineteenth century Russia – and perhaps not as great as the distance between the Dublin literary pubs and the peasantry of Gaelic-speaking Connemara. Hence, also, there was less room for the cultivation of illusion. The gentry lived, for at least a part of the year, on their own estates, and all of their dealings with the people were not mediated by bailiffs or servants. Henry Fielding was not likely to meet a holy peasant any more than his half-brother, the London stipendiary, was likely to meet with a holy highwayman. And if this is accounted a matter of circumstance only, then the profound revaluation of social attitudes entailed in Puritanism gives us the inner evidence. Holy peasants are generally to be found in countries with a Holy Church. Protestant England required, not obedient children, but a sober and industrious poor, informed by an inner discipline.

The English cultural framework of the eighteenth century was that of a realistic paternalism. In individual terms, the expression of this might be repressive or casual or warmly humanitarian: now Squire Western and now Squire Allworthy might show his face. But in general terms, paternalism presumed an essential qualitative difference between the validity of educated experience – polite culture – and the culture of the poor. A man's culture, just as much as his social prestige, was graded according to the hierarchy of rank.

This is not to say that the gentry ignored or despised the culture of the people. On the contrary, many of them were permissive and inquisitive. Some actively favoured popular amusements: found the purses for prize-fights: fought a main of cocks with neighbouring farmers: or did in fact preside over the sports on the village green. Others (like many contributors to the *Gentleman's Magazine*) took time off to observe local customs, record song and ballad, and explore local dialects. The last years of the eighteenth century see that foundation study of English folk-lore, John Brand's *Observations on Popular Antiquities* – itself based on the work of scores of earlier observers. But the note of apology in Brand's Preface is characteristic of the paternalist tone:

> ... nothing can be foreign to our enquiry, much less beneath our notice, that concerns the smallest of the Vulgar; of those little Ones who occupy the lowest place, though by no means of the least importance in the political arrangement of human Beings.

For (Brand also notes) pride and the necessities of civil Polity have 'portioned out the human Genus into ...a variety of different and subordinate Species.' The crucial word is 'subordinate.'[2]

A confirmation of the strength of this paternalist framework can be seen in the manner in which the trickle of poor men of talent was assimilated within it. I am not referring to the authentic popular traditions of folk-song, dialect verse, and so on, but of the 'peasant' poets who were discovered and treated with such insufferable patronage by the eighteenth-century gentry. As early as 1730 the unhappy Stephen Duck, the 'Thresher Poet' was acclaimed and summoned to the presence of Queen Caroline. His patron had the callousness to conceal from him for some days the fact that his wife had died at his home while he was walking to London, for fear that the news might disturb the royal audience. Duck ended up with preferment in the Church, leaving his one good poem in the threshing yard behind him. He was the first of a number. Even the officious Hannah More had her protégée, Ann Yearsley, the Bristol milk-woman, with whom she quarrelled as soon as Ann took a step towards independence. Most talented was Robert Bloomfield, well known as the 'farmer's boy' – although his poem throbs with the nostalgia of a shoemaker's apprentice confined in a London garret workshop. Bloomfield, of course, has many passages which plead the cause of the poor: There are, for example, the reflections which follow upon his description of the traditional harvest-home:

> Such were the days, ...of days long past I sing,
> When Pride gave place to mirth without a sting;
> Ere tyrant custom's strength sufficient bore
> To violate the feelings of the poor;
> To leave them distanc'd in the mad'ning race,
> Where'er refinement shows its hated face:
> Nor causeless hated ...'tis the peasant's curse,
> That hourly makes his wretched station worse;
> Destroys life's intercourse; the social plan
> That rank to rank cements as man to man:
> Wealth flows around him, Fashion lordly reigns;
> Yet poverty is his, and mental pains.[3]

But even such passages as these the frame of paternalism could contain. It was allowable – and even proper in a 'natural' genius who had served as a farmer's boy – to recall the rich to their duties. There is nothing in such a plea which calls in question subordination within the 'social plan'.

It is in the 1790s, under the impact of the French Revolution, the *Rights of Man*, and the political claims of *égalité*, that the whole notion of cultural subordination comes under radical scrutiny. It is interesting to note that the advanced reformers of the time found it more easy to advocate the political programme of equality – manhood suffrage – than they did to shed the cultural attitudes of superiority. John Thelwall – regarded by the orthodox as one of the most notorious Jacobins in England – has a characteristic passage in his *Tribune*: 'I have been rambling, according to my wonted practice, in the true democratic way, on foot, from village to village ...'

> In the course of these rambles I have dropped, occasionally, into the little hedge ale-houses to refresh myself. I have sat down among the rough clowns, whose tattered garments were soiled with their rustic labours; for I have not forgot that all mankind are equally my brethren; and I love to see the labourer in his ragged coat – that is I love the labourer: I am sorry his coat is obliged to be so ragged. I love the labourer then, in his ragged coat, as well as I love the Peer in his ermine; perhaps better ...[4]

And so on. The distance between man and man may no longer be so cold, but it has scarcely begun to be crossed.

But in Thelwall's contemporary and friend, William Wordsworth, we find ourselves, suddenly, in a new situation. There was of course nothing new (if one thinks of *Lyrical Ballads*) in expressing sympathy for the poor – or in taking tales from humble life. There was not even – although here we do tremble on the edge of the real change – anything wholly new in the suggestion that the poor had a vivid and authentic interior life. 'Love, loyalty, and passion such as this' – exclaimed young Werther, after describing the unhappy outcome of a peasant's love for his Mistress – 'live and can be found in all purity among a class of people we like to call uncultivated and crude. We cultured ones – cultured until there is nothing left!'

This kind of sentiment certainly does take us, by a direct road, to Book XII of the *Prelude*:

> When I began to inquire,
> To watch and question those I met, and held
> Familiar talk with them, the lonely roads
> Were schools to me in which I daily read

> With most delight the passions of mankind,
> There saw into the depths of human souls,
> Souls that appear to have no depth at all
> To vulgar eyes. And now convinced at heart
> How little that to which alone we give
> The name of education hath to do
> With real feeling and just sense ...[5]

But even if the road is direct, there is some change: some watershed has been crossed. It is not so much what is said, but the intensity with which it is felt. There is a suspicion that Werther is a *voyeur* into the life of the poor for kicks, whereas we cannot doubt that with Wordsworth the experience is real and central. The passage works precisely by reversing the customary assumptions of the polite culture. Indeed, the word 'vulgar' is so placed as to turn the cultural table round: so that the reader is placed below, with Wordsworth, talking to the common wayfarers on the roads where 'real feeling and just sense' are to be found, condemning the levity and vulgarity of the polite.

This is not a passing insight of Wordsworth's: it is one of the largest, but not the best understood, of the themes presented in the *Prelude*. Criticism, in recent years, has fastened upon so many other matters that it is possible for readers of this great poem to come from it unaware that it is what it is: an affirmation of the worth of the common man, a statement of faith enduring through perplexity and shock in universal brotherhood. 'My present Theme -

> Is to retrace the way that led me on
> Through Nature to the love of Human kind.

Inexorably the theme is worked out, from Wordsworth's unusual dual vantage points in experience: inexorably the cold distance is closed. From one aspect he draws upon his experiences – unusual for his class – of men in the setting of natural activities – his schoolfellows, the shepherds, the Cumberland community. Explicitly he rejects the temptation to fall back into effete pastoral idealizations, or into some Lakeland variant of the holy peasant. 'This Creature -

> Was not a Corin of the groves, who lives
> For his own fancies, or to dance by the hour
> In coronal, with Phillis in the midst,
> But, for the purposes of kind, a man
> With the most common; Husband, Father; learn'd,
> Could teach, admonish, suffer'd with the rest
> From vice and folly, wretchedness and fear ...

From his other vantage point he develops his sense of revolutionary man – the potential in human nature which he had glimpsed in France -

> The soil of common life was at that time
> Too hot to tread upon ...

And, once again,

> ... in rudest men
> Self-sacrifice the firmest, generous love
> And continence of mind, and sense of right
> Uppermost in the midst of fiercest strife.

Recoiling from revolutionary excesses and from his own abstract espousal of Godwinism, Wordsworth nevertheless moves on to the conjuncture of the two strands of experience, when he describes, in Book XII of the *Prelude*, his recourse to the society of common men in his own country:

> ... there I found
> Hope to my hope, and to my pleasure peace,
> And steadiness; and healing and repose
> To every angry passion. There I heard
> From mouths of lowly men and of obscure

A tale of honour.

Once again, 'honour' is a word wrested out of its customary associations in the educated culture and applied in a wider, unfamiliar context. It was in such company that Wordsworth was able to see through all 'the outside marks by which –

> Society has parted man from man
> Neglectful of the universal heart.

This vision into the universal heart – this transmutation of the political claims of *égalité* into the interior life – takes us altogether outside the paternalist framework. It is no momentary insight but a deliberate enduring vision expressed with a philosophic maturity which challenged the received culture. Wordsworth shifted not only his own standpoint but that of those who were to follow. In closing the distance between himself and common men, he aligned himself *with* the common man in sensibility, and opened a distance as between them both and the polite culture. The very word 'common' – 'a Man with the most common' – acquired significantly new notations: we are placed *with* the common as against the culture –

> Of royal Courts, and that voluptuous life
> Unfeeling, where the Man who is of soul
> The meanest thrives the most, where dignity,
> True personal dignity, abideth not,
> A light and cruel world, cut off from all
> The natural inlets of just sentiments,
> From lowly sympathy, and chastening truth ...

Nor is this only the conventional renunciation of power and pelf, although it draws upon that tradition. The values to which we are led are those which belong – with dignity and lowly sympathy – *more* to the common man than to his superiors. Wordsworth overleaps one barrier which had for so long hedged the paternalist value-system about: that of articulateness. He conveys in passage after passage – one thinks of his description of his night-walk over the mountains in the company of the taciturn soldier – a sense of sympathies with those for whom 'words are but under-agents of their souls.'

The Wordsworthian impulse stretches forward across the nineteenth and into the present century. I shall return to this in a moment. But, first, it is necessary to note one of its characteristics. The equality of worth of the common man, which Wordsworth asserted, lay in moral and spiritual attributes, developed through experiences of labour, suffering, and through primary human relationships. It was grounded very much less upon rational attributes, and he was actively distrustful of formal education which might inhibit or divert experiential growth. Faced with a choice between education and experience, Wordsworth would have opted without hesitation for the latter: and, indeed, there are passages in which he seems intent upon forcing exactly this option upon the reader.

In this he was not, of course, representative of the conscience of the upper classes of his time. For the other major impulse which originates in this period and which stretches forward as far as this century is to be found in that set of reactions provoked by fear of the revolutionary potential of the common people. In the counter-revolutionary mood engendered by the French Revolution – and the reform movements in England – paternalism changed its nature and emerged in a meaner, more interfering, and more authoritarian form. In some respects there was an accession of concern on the part of the gentry for the poor: there is little absent-mindedness about the Sunday Schools and the societies for bettering their condition or suppressing their vices. But the emphasis has changed. The old-fashioned paternalist was willing – within defined limits of social order – to allow the poor to get on with living, working, and amusing themselves in the ways which they themselves chose. The evangelical follower of Wilberforce or Hannah More was forever busying himself with social discipline and moral rescue; discriminating between different grades of deserving poor; justifying the outlay of the capital of charity in terms of its rate of interest, as evidenced in greater industry, sobriety, frugality, and obedience. Even the best-intentioned of these reformers saw their ventures as a form of social insurance against popular disturbance. These responses became so deeply embedded in the polite culture that one may see them reactivated again and again during every period of popular unrest in the nineteenth century – during the reform movements of 1819 and 1832, Chartism, the 1880s. They may still be detected in the anxious response of some to the 'problem' of working-class leisure today.

Sadly enough, a representative expression of these attitudes can be found in the early writing of Wordsworth's friend and collaborator, S. T. Coleridge. The daily toil of the labouring poor, he wrote, sinks 'the rational being in the mere animal':

> It is a mockery of our fellow creature's wrongs to call them equal in rights, when by the bitter compulsion of their wants we make them inferior to us in all that can soften the heart, or dignify the understanding.

This is the old view of a 'subordinate' culture; and it is in contradiction to Wordsworth's valuation of the 'real feeling and just sense' of his fellow wayfarers. 'Alas', Coleridge continued: 'between the Parlour and the Kitchen, the Tap and the Coffee-room – there is a gulph not to be passed.' It may at least be allowed that he did not, like John Thelwall, believe that it was to be bridged by political machinery alone. Reformers (he argued) 'must endeavour to diffuse among our domestics those comforts and that illumination which far beyond all political ordinances are the true equalizers of men'.[6] This was written in 1795, at a time when Coleridge was still striving to reconcile his Jacobin sympathies with his intellectual alienation from the common people. Less than ten years later he wrote a much more lamentable letter, whose sentiments are scarcely to be distinguished from those of such condescending paternalists as Hannah More. The occasion was a reply to his friend Thomas Poole, of Stowey, who had written to Coleridge some account of 'servant trouble' in his house:

> As to your servants and the people of Stowey in general (Coleridge replied) you have been often unwisely fretful with me when I have pressed upon you their depravity. Without religious joys and religious terrors, nothing can be expected from the *inferior* classes in society ...[7]

This was a time when even circulating libraries were regarded by good Church and King men as 'among the chief engines of Jacobinism'. This hysteria faded as the threat of French invasion died away: but the more general responses remained: and some of the consequences of the impoverished, mean, anxious and manipulative educational stance which resulted have been ably discussed by Harold Silver, David Owen, Brian Simon and others, and, of course, in the field of nineteenth century adult education by John Harrison.[8] It is not my intention to rehearse the account which they give, but to direct attention to a further consequence – the crippling limitations of attitude which resulted among men of education towards the culture and – for the two are integrally related – the experience of those who stood outside the educated culture.

One may see this clearly if one looks at educated responses towards the traditional entertainments of the people. These responses are all enshrined within a letter published in the *Monthly Magazine* in 1798 from (the *nom de plume* is itself significant) 'A Friend to the innocent Amusements of the industrious Poor':

> Being at present upon a visit at the house of a very respectable friend, who has several large collieries, together with many other extensive undertakings, and whose benevolence is equal to his ability, he told me, that application had just been made to him by a party of his colliers, tenants, labourers, and others, for permission to act a stage-play at their annual feast in August next; but that he had so strongly expressed his disapprobation, that he thought they would relinquish it: adding, however that upon farther consideration, he was doubtful, as they must have some amusements, whether he had not better give his consent to this, as being, upon the whole, less hurtful than some others to which they had been accustomed.
>
> It happened yesterday, that a collier of eminent comic talents, who was at the head of the deputation, and who always at Christmas fills the important place of jester to the morris-dancers, applied to me upon the subject, when the following conversation ensued:
>
> 'Pray, madam, did you hear our master say aught about our acting a play at the feast? He was right angry at me for asking him leave.'
>
> 'I did hear him mention it, James.'
>
> 'And do you think he will let us act?'
>
> 'I really cannot tell. What is the play you would wish to perform?'
>
> 'I am sure I do not know its name, but the first man that speaks they call Sir John: they say there's a deal of sport in it, but no

harm like, or aught of that.'

'How came you, James, to wish to act a play which you have never read?'

'Why, madam, you see, they acted it at F-n, but four miles off, three years ago: they had it from London, and we could get their book.'

'But I am afraid, James, if Mr. M- were to consent, you would all go to the alehouse, as soon as the play was over. You know how much he is your friend, and that he would not deny you any diversion that would not hurt you.'

'Yes, to be sure, madam, and that's it: you may think we used to have cockings, and I was a bit that way myself, Now, thought I, if our master would let us act a play, when then, you see, we should not spend all our money in betting one against another, and in getting drunk.'

'Where would you act your play, in a barn?'

'No, no, on the green, to be sure: we would start about five o'clock in the afternoon, and it would hold us till about eight; for though they say it is but short, yet, you see, we should have our dresses to change like, and then we should have fiddlers, and all would take up time.'

'Well, but Mr. M- fears that the play itself, if, as you say, it has sport in it, might have a tendency to do harm, and to prepare you for following scenes of riot and disorder at the alehouse, whither, after it was over, I still fear, you would go. To be sure, James, you would all of you wish that your wives and daughters, at least, should be modest, chaste, and sober; and then for yourselves, when you come to consider what a great deal of money you had spent, and how much you had injured your families, what a great deal you would have to repent of. Now Mr. M- wishes to save you from all this. You know, James, it is but four days since your neighbour, honest Joseph

18

Braithwait, died of a few hours illness, a complaint in his bowels: he was well on Saturday night, and, to all appearance, as stout and as healthy as any of us; yet, on Sunday night, he was a corpse. Now, James, think, if he had been acting a play, the tendency of which was to deprave both his own mind and the minds of others, and had got drunk after it, spending the money which should have maintained his family for weeks to come; if in these circumstances he had been called to give up his account, think what must have been his condition now! ...'

'How ardently were it to be wished', the correspondent concludes, that the diversions of the poor 'could be so contrived for them, as that they might at the same time be innocent!'

What is crippling about this passage is the fear of popular spontaneities – 'the play ...might have a tendency to do you harm, and to prepare you for following scenes of riot and disorder at the alehouse' – the fear of an authentic popular culture beyond the contrivance and control of their betters. Education and culture, no less than the poor rates, were seen as a dole which might be administered to the people or withdrawn according to their deserts. The desire to dominate and to shape the intellectual and cultural growth of the people towards predetermined and safe ends remains extremely strong right through the Victorian years: and it survives today.

From the 1790s, then, one can see the 'march of intellect', with its mutual improvement societies, its mechanics' institutes, and its Sunday lectures, beginning to move forward: but at the same time, it was leaving behind it the customary experiential culture of the people. I do not wish to suggest that all in this culture was integrated, spontaneous, and admirable. This was not so at all. Today, the best folk songs are revived: but the very much more numerous worst – the cruelly coarse or the merely boring – are lost to view. Or, to put it in the other way, those historians who have viewed eighteenth century popular culture through the eyes of John Wesley have remembered the bull-baitings, the bare-fisted murderous pugilism, the wife-beatings, and bastardy rates, but have forgotten the rush-bearings, the expressive dialect humour, and the harvest homes.

But we need not now take up a position on this difficult question of evaluation to make the point: which is that education appeared not only as a leading towards a new and wider mental universe but also as a leading away from, out of, the universe of experience in which the sensibility was grounded. Moreover, in most areas throughout the nineteenth century, the educated universe was so saturated with class responses that it demanded an active rejection and despisal of the language, customs, and traditions of received popular culture. The self-educated working man who dedicated his nights and his Sundays to the pursuit of knowledge was also asked at every turn to reject the entire human lore of his childhood and of his fellow workers as uncouth, immoral, ignorant.

It is not difficult to understand and to sympathize with the pressures of their position. The realization of the aims of the working-class movement demanded, not only of its leaders, but also of thousands of its ordinary members, new qualities of self-discipline, self-respect, and educated skills. The struggle of the minority was so long and so hard, the periods in which they appeared to have been abandoned by their own class were so frequent, that even the most dedicated tended to look upon their fellow workingmen at times with disgust or despair. After more than forty years of outstanding service, that exceptional leader of the London trade unionists, John Gast, exploded suddenly in 1834 to Francis Place: 'the only way to an Englishman's Brains is through his guts.' 'I myself,' he continued, 'belong to an institution in town which give lectures every Sunday evening, and some times in the week, and we have a good attendance, we are all working men that lecture.' But even so he lamented the ignorance and drunkenness of 'the vulgar and ignorant part of the people':

> Burk was not much out of the way when he called them the Swinish Multitude; for feed a Pig well and you may do anything with him.[9]

Francis Place himself was far more of a prig: his greatest hope for working men was that they should, through the ministrations of the Steam Intellect Society, adopt the style of life and mental habits of the middle class. And an impoverished shadow of exactly this was what formal school education in fact offered to the children of working people until very recent times. The tension was expressed in the very medium of instruction, the language. Hardy was one of the first to explore its meaning:

> Mrs. Durbeyfield habitually spoke the dialect; her daughter (Tess), who had passed the Sixth Standard in the National School under a London-trained mistress, spoke two languages: the dialect at home, more or less; ordinary English abroad and to persons of quality.

Several years ago, before I left Halifax, a respected member of the local labour movement, the late Mr Hanson Halstead – a man with the skills of an engineer who had opted to become a smallholder, a man who – despite his long association with the NCLC and WEA and his extensive political wisdom – had something of the air of a rough countryman, and who always when his intellect was most alert and his insights most swift fell into rich West Riding speech – a man, in fact who seemed to live always in that cultural *Border Country* of which Raymond Williams has written – did me the honour of giving to me a plain Boots diary in which he had set down, in his own style, some chapters of autobiography:

I am not cming to starting work, but had worked since I was 9 years old hawking bread and wot not, we had to pass Standard 2 in those days for Half time, working from 6 o'clock to 12 ...when we got to school a 2 o'clock we used to fall asleep on the desk, and if you had a sensible teacher he used to let you, but if you had a ballie like we had on one occasion it was hell on earth. I used to get the strap every day, must have always been a rebel, but I did not think anything about it ...

After some melancholy descriptions of his teachers, Mr Halstead continues:

We had another Siddaler, Henry Thomas, who used to forget himself and break into our slang many a time in the day if you were outside the class ...Sometimes when he was that way out he would say, narthen lasses and lads, youl just do your composition reight sharp and ...I'll read John Hartleys and being a Siddaler he could because it was written in our language ...The teachers that came from away were always a snooty lot, if you made a slip at all, but how could you help it, when you spoke two languages?

Too often it was not only the teachers but the whole educated culture which seemed to be 'snooty' and which came 'from away'. In 1911 a former Chief Inspector of Schools, Edmond Holmes, launched (in *What is and What Might Be*) a quite devastating attack upon the entire educational process. The attitudes engendered by the Revised Code (payment by results) operating until 1897 (and perpetuated in many schools long after this) aspired to dominate the child:

The aim of his teacher is to leave nothing to his nature, nothing to his spontaneous life, nothing to his free activity; to repress all his natural impulses; to drill his energies into complete quiescence; to keep his whole being in a state of sustained and painful tension. (p. 48)

When the child's spirit was broken and 'he has been reduced

to a state of mental and moral serfdom, the time has come for the system of education through mechanical obedience to be applied to him in all its rigour.' The system he saw as 'an ingenious instrument for arresting the mental growth of the child, and deadening all his higher faculties.' It is a criticism which takes us directly to that other devastating treatment of Board School education, the chapter entitled 'The Man's World' in *The Rainbow*.

I must resume my argument to this point. Attitudes towards social class, popular culture, and education became 'set' in the aftermath of the French Revolution. For a century and more, most middle class educationalists could not distinguish the work of education from that of social control: and this entailed too often, a repression of or a denial of the validity of the life experience of their pupils as expressed in uncouth dialect or in traditional cultural forms. Hence education and received experience were at odds with each other. And those working men who by their own efforts broke into the educated culture found themselves at once in the same place of tension, in which education brought with it the danger of the rejection of their fellows and self-distrust. The tension of course continues still.

But what happened meanwhile to the older impulse of cultural *égalité*, deriving from the same decade, with which Wordsworth was peculiarly identified? The impulse continues of course: one can pick it up at a hundred places in the nineteenth century. Its weakness, perhaps, lay in its tendency to equate the conflict between education and experience as one between intellect (or mere mechanical intellect) and feeling: and, in despair, to overvalue the latter as against the former. One notes this in Borrow: or in Dickens' advocacy of Mr. Sleary's good-hearted circus folk as against the rigorous repression of sensibility of Gradgrind and M'Choakumchild: or even in Edward Carpenter's celebration, in his *Towards Democracy*, of a sexual *égalité* more fundamental than educational attributes. This opposition between the educated, intellectual culture and the culture of experience and sensibility is ever-present in Lawrence; and sometimes it gets out of control and leads in the direction of an ugly celebration of irrationalism. There is a moment, however, in *Sons and Lovers*, when it is held in a fine balance:

> 'You know,' (Paul) said to his mother, 'I don't want to belong to the well-to-do middle class. I like my common people best. I belong to the common people.'
>
> 'But if anyone else said so, my son, wouldn't you be in a tear. You know you consider yourself equal to any gentleman.'
>
> 'In myself,' he answered, 'not in my class or my education or my manners. But in myself I am.'
>
> 'Very well, then. Then why talk about the common people?'
>
> 'Because – the difference between people isn't in their class, but in themselves. Only from the middle classes one gets ideas, and from the common people – life itself, warmth. You feel their hates and loves.'

This is the way in which Lawrence was posing it: education = ideas = middle class: experience ('life itself') = feeling = the common people. As a protest against the 'din-din-dinning' of the Board School, as an affirmation in the face of enervated London literary culture, it is fair enough. But it is scarcely a valid philosophical resolution. Moreover, this kind of attitude can lend support, too easily, to another set of attitudes, strongly present in the working-class movement, about which I have perhaps said too little. The obvious cultural riposte to a class-ridden manipulative educated culture is that of anti-intellectualism: whether militant (as it has appeared at times in the Marxist political tradition) or rancorously bigoted (as in the 'Know Nothing' end of American populism) or wet and self-satisfied and sentimental (as it has appeared, rather more often, in the English nonconformist tradition). This may be seen, indeed, as a peculiarly English vice and I have suggested elsewhere that some part of the blame for it may lie with the Methodist tradition which – while initiating a new impulse of spiritual egalitarianism – nevertheless turned away from the more rigorous intellectual traditions of the earlier dissenting churches. The pure in heart may indeed be blessed: but they may also offer themselves as a fertile pastureland upon which the demagogue and the careerist may safely graze. It may be true and important to insist that we value men not by their class or educational attributes but by their moral worth: but if men – and especially if educationally-disadvantaged men – begin to value themselves too complacently in this way it can serve too easily as an excuse for the giving up of intellectual effort. My fellow tutors here will, I suspect, take the point: they know, only too well, the student to whom I refer. They may also know the tutor who has made himself accomplice to the giving-up, and who has been happy to accept the moral worth of his students in place of their essays. They may even have seen him, as I have, late in the evening, in the mirror.

The problem, then, is difficult. If we really espoused, without further definition, Wordsworth's 'real feeling and just sense' we would not be in the educational business at all: we could leave it to the school of life. There is perhaps only one work in the nineteenth century which fully discloses the complexity, and that is *Jude the Obscure*. The Wordsworthian impulse is there, of course, as it is throughout Hardy, in his sense of the worth of common life. But it would be ridiculous to accuse Hardy of selling the intellectual values short. What is convincing in the novel is the balance of values that is maintained, the dialectical interrelation between intellectual disciplines and 'life itself'. For the story is not simply the one that is too easily recalled to mind in the adult education movement: of the young lad with his Utopian vision of Christminster, as a centre of high disinterested learning: of his efforts at self-education: of his work as a young stonemason in Christminster, rubbing shoulders with the undergraduates who were oblivious to his aspirations:

> He was a young workman in a white blouse, and with stone-dust in the creases of his clothes; and in passing him they did not even see him, or hear him, rather saw through him as through a pane of glass at their familiars beyond.

Nor is it only the story of the closing of the gates of Biblioll College against his aspirations, and the final irony of his death in cheap lodgings in the city of his disenchanted vision. For Hardy insists at every point that it was not only Jude but Christminster itself that was impoverished by his rejection.

It is in the stone-yard that 'for a moment there fell on Jude a true illumination; that here ...was a centre of effort as worthy as that dignified by the name of scholarly study within the noblest of the colleges.' It is not only that the labourers and the scholars are integrally related by economic and social ties: that without 'the manual toilers in the shabby purlieu' of Christminster 'the hard readers could not read nor the high thinkers live.' It is also that it could only be here, in the real context of living experience, that the ideas of the thinkers could be embodied and tested: Jude 'began to see that the town life was a book of humanity infinitely more palpitating, varied, and compendious than the gown life.' In returning to Jude's aspiration a 'freezing negative' the university revealed only its own impoverishment. 'He still thinks,' Sue said to Arabella, 'it a great centre of high and fearless thought, instead of what it is, a nest of commonplace schoolmasters whose characteristic is timid obsequiousness to tradition.'

At some distance opposite, the outer walls of Sarcophagus College – silent, black, and windowless – threw their four centuries of gloom, bigotry, and decay into the little room she occupied, shutting out the moonlight by night and the sun by day.

So that Jude emerges, not just as the victim of an ungenerous system, but as the true protagonist of intellectual and cultural values. Jude and Sue, in their pursuit of new kinds of freedom, comradeship and equality in marriage, are engaged in a pursuit more serious than any exercise of abstracted thought. Their successes lead on to the enhancement of life: their failures are irreparable.

This is not a rejection of educated culture in favour of experience. The vision of Christminster endures with Jude to the end: 'perhaps', he says, 'it will soon wake up and be generous. I pray so!' It is a rejection of the abstraction of intellectual values from the context in which they must be lived, and an affirmation that those who do the living must attain to the intellectual values if they are not to be ground down by 'crookedness, custom, and fear'. We are back where we commenced; with the necessary dialectic of education and experience.

How far is all of this now 'old history'? How far have widening educational opportunities bridged the 'cold distance'? How far have the political and social changes of the past three decades brought us closer to a common culture? Do the themes of this lecture have any continuing relevance in adult education?

At this point, as an experienced tutor, I should evade the issues by announcing the commencement of discussion. But since the formalities of this occasion disallow this familiar exit, I must offer some sketchy suggestions.

Of course, the estrangement of cultures is not now of the same order as it was one hundred years ago. The old parochial popular culture has long crumbled, and the more politically-articulated working-class culture which succeeded it in the industrial centres has also been waning in vitality for two decades. Educationalists have successfully resisted and thrown back – especially in elementary education – the meaner manifestations of cultural domination and social control.

But the impulse towards cultural egalitarianism which I have associated with Wordsworth has for some time been threatened – and, I think, very seriously threatened – from an unexpected direction. The needs of an advanced industrial society, taken together with the dogged pressures of the political labour movement, have greatly enlarged the educational opportunities of the people. But Jude's vision of Christminster has waned in intensity with each advance in educational provision. For education has come to be seen, very widely, and by many working people themselves, simply as an instrument of selective social mobility. Moreover, whatever method of selection occurs, the entire system works in such a way as to confuse certain kinds of intellectual ability (or facility) with human achievement.

Social approval of educational success is marked in a hundred ways: success brings financial reward, a professional style of life, social prestige; it is supported by a whole apologia for modernization, technological necessity, equality of opportunity. It is not necessary to work long inside any university to discover that even the most humane among both staff and student bodies find it an effort not to equate educational achievement with a valuation of human worth. And many of those outside the universities, of those who fail to prove themselves to be sufficiently equal to climb the steps of opportunity, have impressed upon them in contrary ways a sense, not of difference, but of human failure.

Such developments entail a fundamental betrayal of the kind of equality of worth which Wordsworth imagined and which Mansbridge and Tawney worked to bring about. The educated culture is not encapsulated from the culture of the people in the old class-bound ways: but it is encapsulated nonetheless, within its own walls of intellectual self-esteem and spiritual pride.

There are, of course, more people coming within the capsule than ever before. But it is a most serious error – which can only be believed by those who look in upon the universities from outside – to suppose that all within the capsule are the ardent protagonists, in Hardy's sense, of intellectual and cultural value. In the good adult class, the criticism of life is brought to bear upon the work or subject under study. In the nature of the case this is less common with students; and much of the work of the university teacher is that of a kind of intellectual grocer, weighing and measuring out syllabuses, reading-lists, essay-themes, in pursuance of a prescribed professional training.

The danger is that this kind of necessary professional technology will be mistaken for intellectual authority: and that the universities – presenting themselves as a syndicate of all the 'experts' in every branch of knowledge – will expropriate the people of their intellectual identity. And in this they are seconded by the great centralized media of communication – and notably the television – which do in fact often present the academic – or should I say certain photogenic academics? – not as a specialized professional man, but as an 'expert' on life itself in exactly this sense.

The gains of the past decades (for I do not dispute the gains) will only tend in the direction of a common egalitarian culture if the dialectical intercourse between education and experience is maintained and enlarged. And I am arguing this now, less from the standpoint of those outside the universities who stand in need of whatever skills the universities might bring to them, than from the standpoint of those within the universities themselves who stand in need – for their own intellectual health – of the scrutiny and criticism of those without.

At the Oxford Conference of 1907, J. M. Mactavish of the Shipwrights made that notable speech which asserted, not the needs, but the *rights* of those without:

> I claim for my class all the best of all that Oxford has to give. I claim it as a right – wrongfully withheld – wrong not only to us but to Oxford ...Not only are workpeople deprived of the right of access to that which belongs to no class or caste, the accumulated knowledge and experience of the race, but the race loses the services of its best men. I emphasize that point because I wish it to be remembered that workpeople could do far more for Oxford, than Oxford can do for the workpeople. For, remember, democracy will realize itself with or without the assistance of Oxford; but if Oxford continues to stand apart from the workpeople, then she will ultimately be remembered, not for what she is but for what she has been.[10]

Today the matter could no longer be put, with any conviction, in this class-defined and politically-challenging way. But much of what Mactavish was saying remains true. Democracy will realize itself – if it does – in our *whole* society and our *whole* culture: and, for this to happen, the universities need the abrasion of different worlds of experience, in which ideas are brought to the test of life.

The university extra-mural department should, in fact, be – as it has been for so long in the history of this University – one major location of exactly this dialectic: an outlet for knowledge and skills, an inlet for experience and criticism. There may be great changes in the kinds of public with which the department is related: but there should be no changes in the mutuality of this relationship. It cannot perform its function properly (I would suggest) if it becomes too highly professionalized, too much of an annexe of a university. Nor should it capitulate too easily before the temptation of reaching great masses of people which new media – the local radio station or the 'University of the Air' – might provide. Important as these media are, in supplementing traditional provision, their one-way character could strike at the essential reciprocity of the adult class.

I return, in the end, to a simple brief, from which I have been arguing, perhaps obsessively, throughout. It is a brief in which I was well grounded by Professor Raybould when I came to work here with him nearly twenty years ago. There is no automatic correlation between 'real feeling and just sense' and educational attainments. But the pressures of our time are leading us to confuse the two – and university teachers, who are not always noted for their humility, are often ready to assent to the confusion. To strike the balance between intellectual rigour and respect for experience is always difficult. But the balance today is seriously awry. If I have redressed it a little, by reminding us that universities engage in adult education not only to teach but also to learn, then my purpose is fulfilled.

NOTES

1. *Guardian*, 19 May 1967. See also Raymond Williams, 'Thomas Hardy' *Critical Quarterly*, Winter, 1964.
2. John Brand, *Observations on Popular Antiquities* (1813), I, xxi-xxii. Robert Bloomfield, *The Farmer's Boy* (1806 ed.), p. 46.
3. *Tribune* (1796), II, no. xvi, pp. 16-17.
4. All quotations are from the 1805 version of *The Prelude*, ed. E. de
5. Selincourt, Oxford University Press.
6. Samuel Taylor Coleridge, *Conciones ad Populum* (1795), p. 25.
7. Mrs. Henry Sandford, *Thomas Poole and his Friends* (1888), II, pp. 294-6.
8. Harold Silver, *The Concept of Popular Education*, (1965), MacGibbon & Kee; Brian Simon, *Studies in the History of Education, 1780-1870*, (1960), Lawrence and Wishart; Brian Simon, *Education and the Labour Movement, 1870-1920*, (1965), Lawrence and Wishart; David

E. Owen, *English Philanthropy, 1660-1960*, (1965), Harvard University Press; J. F. C Harrison, *Learning and Living, 1790-1960*, (1961), Routledge and Kegan Paul.

9. John Gast to Frances Place, *Brit. Mus. Add. MSS.*, 27, 829, ff. 19-20.

10. Quoted in Albert Mansbridge, *University Tutorial Classes*, p. 194.

DISENCHANTMENT OR DEFAULT?

A LAY SERMON

What has been happening in Wordsworth and Coleridge
scholarship in the past two decades amounts to the patient
restoration of much-defaced portraits; to add to the problem,
these are sometimes self-defaced self-portraits. The work is
painfully difficult. Each year brings some small readjustment
to the record. I cannot even pretend to full information as to
the state of scholarship, although I should acknowledge my
own debt to three scholars whose themes have touched closely
upon my own: Professors Erdman, Schneider, and Woodring.[1]

The restoration has done much already to dispel one
critical stereotype – that Wordsworth the poet begins at the
moment when Wordsworth the politically committed man
ends. This is not the way in which the old scholars – Legouis
or George McLean Harper – used to regard the matter: they
were disposed to see, in the *Prelude*, Wordsworth the
Brissotine or the Foxite Whig. In important respects their
readings were right. In more recent years there has been a
tendency to press the moment of political disenchantment
further and further back, and to present it in a catastrophic
manner, as if, as each area of Wordsworth's political beliefs
suffered disenchantment, it became available to the poetic
sensibility – very much as if his mind were a country occupied
by an oppressive mechanical philosophy, in which one

33

province after another was liberated for 'maturity.'

I don't see things in this way, but to enter into the argument as it relates to the years 1794-1796 would involve too much delay. It is my view (in brief) that one cause of misunderstanding has been an insufficiently close attention to the actual lived historical experience. In default of this, we are sometimes offered a history of ideas which has paid excessive attention to Godwinism, as if it were the only authentic set of republican ideas available.

I don't dispute that the phase in which Wordsworth espoused the ideas of Godwin and then rejected some part of them was accompanied by intellectual crisis. But the rejection of Godwin was accompanied by a rejection of a mechanical psychology and an abstract enthronement of reason, but not by any rejection of republican ardour. It signalled also – a central theme of the *Prelude* – a turning toward real men and away from an abstracted man.

It is a move away from the *déraciné* Godwinian intelligentsia but toward the common people. The feeling attached to the word 'common' is extraordinarily important in this phase of the poet's development. Coleridge, in one phase of his oscillatory moods, had long been disposed to idealize the values of simple community. The lines leap out of 'Religious Musings' -

> Return, pure Faith! return, meek piety!
> The kingdoms of the world are yours: each heart
> Self-governed, the vast Family of Love
> Rais'd from the common earth by common toil,
> Enjoy the equal produce ...

– lines which the editor of *The Watchman* thought well enough of to extract and publish. The importance of the connotations of 'common' to Wordsworth, in particular in Book II of the *Prelude* (1805), should be too familiar to require repetition. This is one of the bridges from Jacobinism and utopian communism to nature. It is one of the reasons why Hazlitt was right to describe Wordsworth's as a levelling muse, and to make the point again in his review of the *Excursion:*

> Here are no dotted lines, no hedgerow beauties, no box-tree borders, no gravel walks, no square mechanic inclosures; all is left loose and irregular in the rude chaos of aboriginal nature.

Whenever we attempt to define the romantic nature it is always helpful to enquire to what this nature is being opposed, what is not nature.

The break with Godwinism, then, was accompanied by a movement away from abstraction and toward 'enthusiasm.' In Coleridge's case the movement, although crablike, was in 1795-1796 explicitly political. In his Watchman year he was certainly thought to be one of the most dangerous Jacobins in the West Country. And if his friends – and his enemies – and his wife – all thought he was this, then it becomes a little precious to write it down on the grounds of the luminous ambiguities which already accompany his thoughts. In the case of 'Alfoxden's musing tenant' – as Thelwall described Wordsworth in 1797 – there is already a certain transposition of enthusiasm from overtly political to more lowly human locations. It was because the objective political referents appeared unworthy that it also seemed to be important to locate the aspirations of fraternité and égalité in more universal, less particular – and therefore less fragile – referents.

The original of Margaret in 'The Ruined Cottage' was taken (I assume) from Southey's 'Joan of Arc': the passage treats of the death of a common soldier:

> Of unrecorded name
> Died the mean man, yet did he leave behind

One who did never say her daily prayers
Of him, forgetful; who to every tale
Of the distant war lending an eager ear,
Grew pale and trembled. At her cottage door
The wretched one shall sit, and with dim eye
Gaze o'er the plain, where on his parting steps
Her last look hung. Nor ever shall she know
Her husband dead, but tortured with vain hope
Gaze on ...

Earlier still, Coleridge had tried the same theme, with Gothic effects:

O wretched Widow who in dreams dost view
Thy Husband's mangled corpse – and from short doze
Start'st with a shriek! or in thy half-thatched cot,
Wak'd by the wintry night-storm, wet and cold,
Cowr'st o'er thy screaming baby ...

In both of these, she is an explicit text against war. Wordsworth's Margaret remains this, notably in the early versions. But she is also a great deal more. The poem has leaped out of the rigid framework of paternalistic sensibility, in which the interior life of the poor cannot be handled, unless with condescension or as picturesque. It was the transposed Jacobin impulse of *égalité* which broke out of the paternalistic frame.

The impulse is transmuted in some way – from abstract political right to something more local, but also more humanly engaged. This creative moment might be defined as a Jacobinism-in-recoil or a Jacobinism-of-doubt. I must insist upon both sides of this definition. It is no good if we see only the recoil, or the doubt: yet so obsessed was a recent generation of critics with similar experiences of disenchantment in their own time, that this has been the tendency. The doubt is interesting and reputable; the affirmation can be discounted.

But it is exactly within this conflict – the moment when the received culture was challenged, all conventions were called into question, and the great humanist affirmations were abroad, but when sharp experience had shown that the florid periods of the platform Jacobin or the abstract periods of the *philosophes* were inadequate – it is exactly within this conflict that the great romantic impulse came to maturity.

Wordsworth and Coleridge were caught in the vortex of contradictions which were both real and ideal. They were champions of the French Revolution and they were sickened by its course. They were isolated as Jacobins and they abominated Godwinian abstraction. They had broken out of the received culture and they were appalled by some features of the new. They wished to espouse the cause of the people, and they were afraid that the mob might turn first on men of their kind. There is a search for a synthesis at a moment of arrested dialectic; a coruscation of perceptions coming from this tension; a fiery alternating current passing backward and forward between Hartley and Berkeley, Godwin and Burke, Newton and the Book of Revelation, leaving that medley of insights and nonsense which Coleridge was to try all his life to gather into a system.

The theme of this lecture is apostasy and disenchantment. There is a difference between the two. My argument is: the creative impulse came out of the heart of this conflict. There is a tension between a boundless aspiration – for liberty, reason, *égalité*, perfectibility – and a peculiarly harsh and unregenerate reality. So long as that tension persists, the creative impulse can be felt. But once the tension slackens, the creative impulse fails also. There is nothing in disenchantment inimical to art. But when aspiration is actively denied, we are at the edge of apostasy, and apostasy is a moral failure, and an imaginative failure. In men of letters it often goes with a peculiar disposition toward self-bowdlerization, whether in Mr. Southey or in Mr.

Auden. It is an imaginative failure because it involves forgetting – or manipulating improperly – the authenticity of experience: a mutilation of the writer's own previous existential being. In a notable passage in his essay 'On Consistency of Opinion' (1821), Hazlitt commented that there need be no objection to a man's changing his opinions. But:

> he need not ...pass an act of attainder on all his thoughts, hopes, wishes, from youth upwards, to offer them at the shrine of matured servility: he need not become one vile antithesis, a living and ignominious satire on himself.

Coleridge fell into this phase soonest. He had always contained this ambiguity – this sense of shifty foundations, this manner of modifying (almost helplessly) his views to suit an audience – of trying out phrases before he knew whether they were apt. Writing to Lloyd's father in October, 1796, and wanting to reassure him, he tentatively tried out a notorious phrase: 'I have ...snapped my squeaking baby-trumpet of sedition, and have hung up its fragments in the chamber of Penitences.' Meanwhile he was writing – for at least two years – in a very different tone to John Thelwall and other radical friends. The phrase was not fully sounded until March, 1798: 'I have snapped my squeaking baby-trumpet of Sedition & the fragments lie scattered in the lumber-room of Penitence. I wish to be a good man & a Christian – but I am no Whig, no Reformist, no Republican ...' Once again he was writing to a correspondent, brother George in holy orders, who wished to hear from him exactly this. And already the phrase had an uncomfortable apostate air about it. Why the 'squeaking baby-trumpet'? Why defecate upon an enthusiasm whose ink has not yet dried?

Five years later he wrote an extraordinary letter to Sir George and Lady Beaumont. I can't be so sadistic as to invite historians to study it: it is altogether too torturing, too much like an experiment in historical weightlessness. But critics and psychologists should certainly give the letter more attention. It was written under the stress of strong feelings about the execution of the Irish patriot Emmett, whose heroism seemed to call in question Coleridge's self-confidence.

> I have been extremely affected by the death of young Emmett – just 24! – at that age, dear Sir George! I was retiring from Politics, disgusted beyond measure by the manners & morals of the Democrats, & fully awake to the inconsistency of my practice with my speculative Principles. My speculative Principles were wild as Dreams – they were 'Dreams linked to purposes of Reason'; but they were perfectly harmless – a compound of Philosophy & Christianity ...

> ... tho' I detested Revolutions in my calmer moments, as attempts that were necessarily baffled & made blood-horrible by the very causes, which could alone justify Revolutions (I mean, the ignorance, superstition, profligacy, & vindictive passions, which are the natural effects of Despotism & false Religion) – and tho' even to extravagance I always supported the Doctrine of absolute unequivocal non-resistance – yet with an ebullient Fancy, a flowing Utterance, a light & dancing Heart & a disposition to catch fire by the very rapidity of my own motion, & to speak vehemently from mere verbal associations, choosing sentences & sentiments for the very reason, that would have made me recoil with a dying away of the Heart & an unutterable Horror from the actions expressed in such sentences & sentiments – namely, because they were wild, & original, & vehement & fantastic! – I aided the Jacobins, by witty sarcasms & subtle reasonings & declamations full of genuine feeling against all Rulers & against all established Forms! ...

> ... fortunately for me, the Government, I suppose, knew that both Southey & I were utterly unconnected with any party or club or society – (& this praise I must take to myself, that I disclaimed all these Societies, these Imperia in Imperio, these

> Ascarides in the Bowels of the State, subsisting on the
> weakness & diseasedness, & having for their final Object the
> Death of that State, whose Life had been their Birth & growth,
> & continued to be their sole nourishment – . All such Societies,
> under whatever name, I abhorred as wicked Conspiracies ...

We must remember that Coleridge was already a sick man
when he wrote this letter, subject to laudanum, oppressed with
a sense of creative impotence. Recalling all this, we may be
inclined to forgive him. He was always a man whose intellect
was only fitfully within his own control. But we cannot
forgive any critic or historian who accepts such a letter as this
as a true record of any part of his evolution.

With Wordsworth matters are unclear for different
reasons. We have no consecutive epistolary record of his
evolution. He was always disinclined to extend himself in
letters, and if he had seditious sentiments we should not
necessarily expect to find them entrusted to the post.
Reformers knew very well that the mails could be tampered
with. 'Seal your letters first with a wafer, & then some good
wax over it,' Thelwall impressed upon a corespondent in
March, 1794:

> Get good wax! get good wax! When rogues & robbers are in
> authority every man ought to keep a good lock upon his door.

In January, 1795, George Cumberland wrote to his brother
Richard asking urgently for the return of his outspoken letters,
not by post but in a deal box by the wagon:

> My reason ...you will scarcely want an explanation of in these
> times, when we are likely soon to live under an absolute
> Government & be plunged in a Civil War.

As early as May, 1794 (when the Treason Trials were
initiated), Dorothy Wordsworth reassured brother Richard as

to 'William's caution about expressing his political opinions.' The continued problems of communication with Annette would, in any case, have made the mails a sensitive area.

This is at best negative evidence. It warns us only against assuming that Wordsworth had lost his political interests because these are not clearly disclosed in his letters. The evidence of his poetry indicates that, for him, the moment of tension – of Jacobin affirmation and recoil – was far more protracted than it was for Coleridge. Moreover, he had that extraordinary faculty of recollecting earlier emotional states – of musing over them – that tenacity of truth toward them. Nevertheless, with him also the tension eventually slackened, and was followed by his rapid reabsorption into the traditional culture. By the end of the wars, disenchantment had given way to apostasy.

What happened? What made it happen? I can only offer some impressions. And to do this I must pitch you into a close historical context.

Historians, no less than poets and critics, have their 'spots of time.' I want to focus upon two spots, whose significance radiates forward and backward. Both come from the years 1797-1798, with the poets at Stowey and Alfoxden. Both must be seen within the climate of Jacobinism, isolated, the subject of unceasing external vigilance and yet at the same time of inward recoil and confusion – the moment at which the *Lyrical Ballads* were written, the early draft of 'The Ruined Cottage,' and possibly some passages which were to find their way into the *Prelude*.

The first 'spot of time' is in July and August, 1797, when John Thelwall visited the poets, closely followed by the spy Walsh. May I briefly run over some of the incidents in the case, which is often treated as a literary 'humour'? The report had been sent to London not, in the first place, from the gentry, but from the common people. It was a servant at

41

Alfoxden who complained that French people were plotting in the countryside and – worse – washing and mending clothes on the Sabbath day. 'Christopher Trickis and his wife who live at the Dog Pound at Alfoxton told Moggs that the French people had taken the plan of their house.' The first thing which the government agent Walsh heard when he came posting down to Somerset was a conversation in the Globe public bar. A man asked the landlord if Thelwall was gone. The reply was that 'he had been down some time, and that there were a Nest of them at Alfoxton House who were protected by a Mr. Poole.' They were not French, said the landlord, 'but they are people that will do as much harm as all the French can do.' 'The inhabitants of Alfoxton House,' Walsh said in his next report, 'are a Sett of violent Democrats.'

From one aspect that year, 1797-1798, seems idyllic; it was the year that Lloyd and Lamb, Hazlitt and Mackintosh, and other friends, came in to Stowey. There is a glow of warmth, an intensity of communication, an absence of reserve, which Hazlitt recalled:

> Somehow that period ...was not a time when nothing was given for nothing. The mind opened and a softness might be perceived coming over the hearts of individuals, beneath the 'scales that fence' our self-interest.

On the other hand it was a time of terrible isolation – an isolation which perhaps gave an added intensity to the radiance of communication of the brotherhood excluded from the consensus. For Hazlitt's remembered 'softness' was in the midst of hardening hostility, a watchful people, the attention of the gentry and of the Duke of Portland himself.

Mrs. Moorman has found the spy story 'an extremely funny one,' and so, in retrospect, it is. But when our sides have stopped shaking we might question the adequacy of such a judgment as this one, from another noted Wordsworthian scholar, upon John Thelwall's part in the story:

> Actually he was a harmless, kind-hearted man, distinguished in
> later life as a teacher of elocution who specialized in the
> correction of stammering.

It is not, surely, Thelwall's later life and reputation, but his
position in 1797, which should command our attention.

He was at this moment the most notorious public Jacobin
in England. You will find him there, in the plates of Gillray
and lesser cartoonists, generally flourishing a butcher's knife
or raising the torch of arson in his hand. He had been, also, in
1795-1796, the most important link figure between the Jacobin
intellectuals and the plebeian Corresponding Societies.
Throughout 1795 he had lectured to audiences of hundreds in
Beaufort Buildings, off the Strand, publishing his lectures next
year in the *Tribune*. One clause in the Two Acts had been
specifically aimed at political lecturers – in the first place at
Thelwall.

The Two Acts were largely effective. The membership of
the corresponding societies, swelling rapidly at the end of
1795, fell away even more rapidly. The clubs were infested
with spies. The missionaries of the London Corresponding
Society were arrested. One of the last men to attempt a public
Jacobin presence in 1796 was Thelwall. I don't wish to paint
out the warts on the face of an English Jacobin tribune. He
relished notoriety and he was self-dramatizing, but he rode
those difficult years from 1794 to 1796 well. He was
energetic, both politically and intellectually ('energetic
activity of mind and of heart is his master feature,' Coleridge
wrote), he was sometimes judicious, and when supported and
at the centre of the stage, he was a man of courage. His
Tribune lectures give you the energy and attack. His *Rights of
Nature*, which Coleridge at the time thought 'the best
pamphlet that has been written since the commencement of the

war,' gives you the rights of man enlarged into more searching areas of social criticism. His prison poems of 1794 – alack! – give you the postures of the people's tribune. So does this passage in a letter to his wife, in which he describes the reception of his lectures in 1795:

> Two lectures, in particular ...have shaken the pillars of corruption till every stone of the rotten edifice trembled. Every sentence darted from breast to breast with electric contagion, and the very aristocrats themselves – numbers of whom throng to hear me – were frequently compelled by irresistable impulse to join in the acclamations ...

In 1796 he defied the Two Acts, continuing to lecture, but under the disguise of Roman history. Young Crabb Robinson attended one of his lectures, on the elective franchise of the Romans, in June:

> He certainly possesses great address in producing through the medium of another country the very spirit of our own Institutions which it might be dangerous openly to publish.

But in his manner 'I did not see that republican simplicity of Manners & Ideas which I wish to see universally spread.' Robinson's Tory friend, Amyot, has more withering comments about a lecture, in the same month, in Norwich:

> He raves like a mad Methodist parson: the most ranting Actor in the most ranting Character never made so much noise as Citizen Thelwall ...If it had not been for the feebleness of his Person, I sh'd almost have been led to suspect he was going to beat his audience out of doors.

But even Amyot 'was well satisfied with the arrangement & style of his composition.'

I want to insist: Thelwall's defiance of the Two Acts was a national event, a talking-point in the taverns and coffee houses. Even the King was informed of his lectures. Since the forces of law found it difficult to penetrate the disguise of a Roman toga – even though all England knew that he wore a flamboyant cap of liberty upon his head – the forces of order moved in. The lecture tour in East Anglia was brought to an abrupt end. Church-and-Kings thugs mobbed his meetings with impunity. The magistrates refused redress or protection. On one occasion the crew of a man-of-war were given shore leave – and bludgeons with which to enjoy their night out. More than twenty years later Thelwall was still smarting under the 'long series of unparalleled and almost incredible persecutions' of that year, when (he recalled in 1819) he had been:

> proscribed and hunted – driven like a wild beast, and banished like a contagion, from society – during those reiterated attempts by armed banditti to kidnap and murder him ...during all those monstrous atrocities at Yarmouth, at Wisbeach, at Derby, on the borders of Leicestershire – at Stockport and at Norwich ...he never did desert the public – the public deserted him.

It was in this year – in April, 1796 – that the correspondence between Thelwall and Coleridge commenced. Thelwall is generally sold short by the critics, although Professor Woodring has restored the balance. The correspondence, he has wisely noted, was 'warm, honest, and mutually enlarging. It elicited letters the most interesting intellectually, the most secure emotionally, and yet morally the most admirable, of any Coleridge wrote before the age of thirty.' He has left me no more to say on this point, but something might be added about the influence of the correspondence upon Thelwall. It was, I would suggest, heartening in the extreme to the Jacobin in this time of increasing isolation to receive fresh moral supplies from the West Country. Coleridge, with his lectures and his *Watchman,* was a sort of little Bristol Thelwall: the Two Acts caught him also in their toils, and he played with the idea that the special clause against lecturers was aimed at him also. The line in Coleridge's unpublished sonnet to Thelwall -

> Thou, mid thickest fire
> Leap'st on the perilous wall

- Thelwall found to be 'as poetical as it is gratifying.' He would scarcely have been human if he had found it otherwise. Nor did Thelwall by any means get the worst of the correspondence. In his criticism of *Religious Musings* he put his finger unerringly upon one of the worst of its many appalling lines: 'Ye petrify the inbrothell'd Atheist's heart.' It is (he wrote) 'one of those illiberal & unfounded calumnies with which *Christian meekness* never yet disdained to supply the want of argument.' But his conclusion may savour somewhat of patronage:

> While I was yet a Christian & a very zealous one, i.e. when I was about your age, I became thoroughly convinced that Christian poetry was very vile stuff – that religion was a subject which none but a rank infidel could handle poetically
> ...

As one by one all his resources, political, financial, and personal, gave way, his mind turned increasingly to Coleridge, and to the possibility of finding some congenial retreat. In February of 1797 he wrote to a friend that Coleridge was 'one of the most extraordinary Geniuses & finest scholars of the age.' In April Crabb Robinson met him in Thomas Hardy's shop and 'eulogised Burke.' Thelwall

> allowed his transcendant genius but affirmed there were Lumin[ous Starlets] rising above the Horizon who bid fair to eclipse the dazzling splendour of Mr. Burke's Orb. I understand that Coleridge & Southey were the *Starlets* ...

Let us return to our spot of time: Stowey in July of this year. Yes, yes, Thelwall, when he set off on the pedestrian excursion which led to Stowey, was in retreat, but he had reason to be in retreat, and he was not in retreat all that *much*. The business of the spy turns out to be not all that funny after all. The most notorious, if defeated, Jacobin in England was moving west, and he was being *watched*. Coleridge and Wordsworth must have known perfectly well that he was being watched, but gave him the welcome of a comrade and a citizen nonetheless. Nor was this welcome forced. The letter which Citizen John wrote from Stowey to his female Citizen (in apostate's language, his wife) is the happiest, most relaxed letter of his which I have read. He had passed through Bristol on his way, where he had 'met with some enthusiasm, & some *solid* friendship.' He had promised the radicals that he would return to Bristol after visiting Stowey and before moving on to Wales. He even hoped, from lectures and the sale of pamphlets, to raise some money to repair his broken finances:

> But profit & everything else but my Stella & my Babes are now banished from my mind by the enchanting retreat (the Academe of Stowey) from which I write this, & by the delightful Society of Coleridge & of Wordsworth ...

The three men had been rambling 'along a wild romantic dell in these grounds.' 'There have we ..., a literary & political triumvirate,

> passed sentence on the productions and characters of the age – burst forth in poetical flights of enthusiasm & philosophised our minds into a state of tranquility which the leaders of nations might envy and the residents of Cities can never know.

The poem which he wrote after leaving Stowey is among the best three or four which he ever wrote:

47

Ah! let me, far in some sequester'd dell,
Build my low cot; and happy might it prove,
My Samuel! near to thine, that I might oft
Share thy sweet converse, best-belov'd of friends! -
Long-lov'd ere known: for kindred sympathies
Link'd, tho far distant, our congenial souls ...

And 'twould be sweet,
When what to toil was due, to study what,
And literary effort, had been paid,
Alternate, in each other's bower to sit,
In summer's genial season; or, when, bleak,
The wintry blast had stripp'd the leafy shade,
Around the blazing hearth, social and gay,
To share our frugal viands, and the bowl
Sparkling with home-brew'd beverage: – by our sides
Thy Sara, and my Susan, and, perchance,
Allfoxden's musing tenant, and the maid
Of ardent eye, who, with fraternal love,
Sweetens his solitude ...

The Mayor of Bristol, learning of Thelwall's intended return, and of the plans of the Bristol radicals to hold a meeting for him (despite the Two Acts), was a good deal less happy, and wrote urgently to the Duke of Portland for advice. 'Accustomed as I am to the activity and industry of Thelwall and his associates,' the Duke replied on August 7, nevertheless:

> I must own, that I did not expect to receive the intelligence you have sent me, and to hear that a *second* Trial was making to promote a general and publick meeting in your City.

He relied on the firmness of the local authorities to see that the conspiracy was nipped in the bud.

This, then, is to fill in a little the calm background of rural retirement out of which the *Lyrical Ballads* came. The coda to that episode is too well known to bear repeating. An offer by Wordsworth to share Alfoxton House with Thelwall resulted only in notice being served upon the Wordsworths that they could not renew their lease after its expiry in the summer of 1798. Despite Coleridge's earnest attempts, no house could be rented for the defeated agitator near Stowey. If Poole attempted to find Thelwall a house, Coleridge wrote:

> the whole Malignity of the Aristocrats will converge to him ...You cannot conceive the tumult, calumnies, & apparatus of threatened prosecutions which this event [i.e., Wordsworth's presence] has occasioned round about us. If you too should come, I am afraid that even riots & dangerous riots might be the consequence.

I notice that the author of a recent book, *The Making of the English Working Class*, tends to sneer at the sincerity of Coleridge's professions at this point. If he had speculated less, and carried his research a little further, he would have been of a different opinion. Coleridge was sincere. Those riots could have happened.

Thelwall, in any case, had come to know Coleridge well enough on his brief visit to understand his enthusiastic ebullitions with affectionate good humour. In March, 1798, he was writing to Dr. Crompton, speculating upon whether or not Coleridge had accepted the ministry at Shrewsbury:

> I know his aversion to preaching God's holy word for hire, which is seconded a little I suspect by his repugnance to all regular routine & application – I also hope he did not, for I know he cannot preach very often, without travelling from the pulpit to the Tower. Mount him but upon his darling hobby horse, 'the republic of God's own making,' & away he goes like hey go mad, spattering & splashing thro thick & thin & scattering more *levelling* sedition, & constructive treason, than poor *Gilly* or myself ever dreamt of.

The reference to Gilly (Gilbert Wakefield) takes us to our second 'spot of time,' the spring of 1798. Our first spot has illustrated how the democrats, in 1797, were being driven into small and personal survival groups. This helps us to understand something of the forms of their writing: the personal dialogue with one intimate friend gives us the form of the *Prelude*; the interior monologue of the isolated man gives us something of the form of Blake's prophetic books. This isolation did not relax in 1798. This was the year of the Irish rebellion; the year of the first execution in England for treason; the year of heightened invasion threat, especially in the early months of the year – perhaps (with Ireland in revolt) the greatest opportunity for invasion which the French were to have. 'Such a militarily critical moment,' the author of a study of Wordsworth's politics has written, 'was enough to bring any Jacobin to his senses.'

This is not, perhaps, a wholly adequate historical judgment. After all, the notion that the visionaries had only to be 'brought to their senses' is close to those of the contributors to the *Anti-Jacobin Review*, whose merciless lampoons – to which any reply was becoming increasingly treasonable – commenced in 1797. Other modes of bringing men to their senses were employed by the Government throughout March and April. The moves against the press in March have been detailed by Professor Erdman. In April, 1798, the surviving members of the committee of the London Corresponding Society were rounded up, many of them to be held in jail for two years without trial. At the moment when the Bow Street runners burst in upon them they were arguing passionately whether or not to advise their members to join the Volunteers. A small number of those outside the prisons joined a pro-Gallican Irish underground; a few fled to France; very many more abandoned the universal sympathies of earlier years and submerged them in the diminished sympathies of a war of national defence. In the transition, the notations of the word 'patriotism' underwent a great change. Among those who effected an early reconciliation with the establishment was the poet's quarrelsome friend Charles Lloyd, who earned the commendation of the *Anti-Jacobin Review* for some verses in which, with true apostate gusto, he denounced democratic sympathies scarcely a year old:

> 'Twould revoke
> The judgement and the privilege annex'd
> To wealth, and talents, influence, and power!
> 'Twould snatch the promised blessing from the poor,
> Hatching an obstinate sedition
> From pamper'd lust and infidel despair:
> And blot out from its calendar of grace
> Faith and forbearance.

What *were* the alternatives that were open to the English democrats in 1798? 'To defend the Bible in this year 1798 would cost a man his life. The Beast & the Whore rule without control.' This is Blake's annotation on the front of Bishop Watson's *Apology for the Bible* – Watson's reply to Paine's *Age of Reason*. It reminds us that between pro-Gallican conspiracy and patriotic national unity, there were other possible positions, one of which found a poignant expression at this time.

Richard Watson, the Bishop of Llandaff, weaves his flatulent way through this romantic story, a shoddy thread upon which the beads of other men's ardour are strung. A man of the Cambridge enlightenment – a capable professor of chemistry and one of the Whig connection – he was the first of that circle to renounce his democratic professions and to make acceptable terms for himself with the establishment. As Bishop of Llandaff he was an absentee; he was also a pluralist, holding the livings of the archdeaconry of Ely, the rectorship of Carstil, and the vicarage of Somersham. He lived, more than comfortably, in Westmoreland, or at his London house, drawing also the income of the Regius Professorship of Divinity, the duties of which were performed by a *locum tenens*. This was a certain Dr. Kipling (a critic described his lectures: 'his scanty portion of exploded divinity, disguised in barbarous Latin') who had taken the leading part as prosecutor during the expulsion of the reformer William Frend at Cambridge. It was the Bishop's sermon 'The Wisdom and Goodness of God in having made both Rich and Poor' which had driven Wordsworth to write his unpublished 'Letter to the Bishop Llandaff' in 1793. It was the Bishop's *Apology for the Bible* which Blake annotated with such fury, adding, however: 'I have been commanded from Hell not to print this, as it is what our Enemies wish.'

There was, however, one man in England so ill-advised, so immature in his sensibility, as to disregard the commands of hell. He is a man whose importance, in its bearing upon both Coleridge and Blake, has received too little attention. Gilbert Wakefield, the Unitarian divine, was esteemed as – next to Porson – the leading classical scholar of a classical age. He had been a teacher at the Dissenting Academy at Hackney, where Hazlitt was later a scholar. He was not one of those Socinians who brought to Coleridge's mind the image of cold moonlight, for some strange stove raged inside him. Highly unorthodox, he had not however taken to the Godwinian and free-thinking path but had published his own expostulatory reply to Paine's *Age of Reason*.

Wakefield happened to see a copy of the Bishop's latest production – *Address to the People of Great Britain* – at a friend's house. 'He twice picked it up and read a few pages':

> It occurred to him, as he walked home, that it would be no useless, nor unimportant, employment to spend a few hours in

attempting to refute doctrines which appeared to him not merely erroneous but of pernicious tendency.

His reply was written through the night and the next morning; by the afternoon it had gone to the printer.

It was an ill-advised piece of writing, most improper from the pen of an objective scholar. It is disfigured by the *argumentum ad hominem*, which, while no doubt justified in the pages of the *Anti-Jacobin Review*, is of course indecent when addressed not to a hominem but to a bishop. Moreover, Wakefield's arguments were intemperate. He was convinced that peace with France could have been made in 1796, and that the continuance of the war should be laid at the door of those who followed Burke in refusing all treaty with an 'armed doctrine.' It is an interesting point. Wakefield, in fact, was almost certainly right, but that is no excuse for discussing it in terms such as these: 'the genuine professor of the gospel ...contemplates an instigator of war, with his associates and abettors, as an incarnate Satan in the pandemonium of infernal spirits.'

There was worse. There is one point only at which civilian patriotism quails and that is the point at which wars have to be paid for. The Bishop had dared to advocate an income tax of 1/10th – an unpopular measure with the middle classes and lesser gentry, many of whom argued that the tax should be graduated according to income. The Bishop, in defence of his proposal, pointed out how much he would suffer under it himself: 'with a family of 8 children I shall feel its pressure as much as most men.' He was led from this to one of his most apt ornamental metaphors:

When all the members of a community are proportionably reduced ...the individuals themselves will feel no elevation or depression in the scale of society. When all the foundations of a great building sink uniformly, the symmetry of the parts is not injured; the pressure on each member remains as it was – no rupture is made: the building will not be so lofty, but it may stand on a better bottom.

Alas! commented the ill-bred Wakefield:

the *groundfloor* of this grand and stable edifice, where myself and my mess-mates of the *swinish multitude* were regaling ourselves ...is sunk for-ever in damps and darkness; only to make ...a more firm foundation for our aristocratical and prelatical superiors, who are frisking and feasting in the upper rooms with ...their customary unconcern.

If a man could speak like this to a bishop, is there any wonder that he could betray his country? He showed the lamentable lack of realism of the disaffected, displaced intellectual. He attacked even the British cabinet:

...the death of a fellow-creature is no more to them, than the fall of an autumnal leaf in the pathless desert; ...they have engendered sham plots, false alarms ...to establish ...their own power by a military despotism over England, like that which now tramples bleeding Ireland ...they have persecuted unto death, they have exiled to the ends of the world, and they now emprison with inconceivable rigour ...their fellow-citizens for trivial offences ...

Wakefield did not proclaim uncritical admiration for the French. He opined that war was nourishing among the French nation a gathering desire 'to return to their vomit' – the same unremarkable (but unmistakable) image which, we remember, Wordsworth was later to use. But if the French could land 60,000 men in England (which he doubted), then 'the kingdom would be lost for ever' because of the 'degree of poverty & wretchedness in the lower orders' which gave them no reasons for attachment to the constitution.

It was at this point that Wakefield lost all touch with

either good taste or loyalty. The Bishop had touched, modestly, upon his own personal courage in daring to declare himself an enemy of France at a time when a successful invasion might result in personal retribution:

> I might have concealed my sentiments, and waited in retirement, till the struggle had been over, and the issue known; but I disdain safety accompanied with dishonour.

He was ready to 'hazard everything in the defence of the country.' 'I am not one of those,' remarked Wakefield,

> so very loyal and so very honest, as the Bishop of Llandaff. My life and my books are all the personalities that I value: and neither of them ...shall be hazarded in defence of the present administration. If the French come, they shall find me at my post, a watchful sentinel in my proper box, MY STUDY ...

Wakefield's was almost the last public voice out of Jacobin England. He was imprisoned, of course; so was his publisher; so was his bookseller, Johnson, that fascinating central figure, a link between Wordsworth and Blake, Mary Wollstonecraft and Coleridge; so was Benjamin Flower, the editor of the *Cambridge Intelligencer*, the last national organ of intellectual Jacobinism; he was imprisoned, for contempt, by the House of Lords, for writing in his paper of the 'Right Reverend time-server and apostate.' George Dyer was also imprisoned, for coming to Flower's defence. The cases ricocheted off each other through 1798 and into 1799. It was, if put together with Professor Erdman's account of the muzzling of the London press, a very efficient mopping-up operation, indeed, of the main centres of opposition among the democratic intelligentsia. Wakefield emerged from prison with weakened constitution two years later, to die at once of fever. More than one subsequent historian has endorsed the judgment of the courts. As Professor Carless Davis noted in his *Age of Grey and Peel*, Wakefield 'represented no one and was a little mad.'

How far does this story connect with the predicament of Wordsworth and Coleridge in the early months of 1798? At every point, I would suggest. I have only time to insist how far the poets were immersed within this total context. Even the lanes around Stowey and Alfoxton resounded with tramping feet, clumsy and histrionic no doubt, but rural England can be a clumsy and stupid place. March and April, 1798, saw the greatest *levée* of the Volunteers in the whole decade. Most local volunteer corps were founded with some little oratorical flourish, some resolution of loyalty, but the North Petherton Corps, which drew upon the services of those who lived in Stowey, was founded in April with a quite unusual flourish of patriotic combat:

> England was never in more imminent danger of being invaded and by an enemy the most barbarous, sanguinary and destructive, than at this present moment, an enemy that has spread desolation, that has been guilty of every enormity, that has spared no one of whatever way of thinking or acting from rapacity and plunder, an enemy that neither the aged matron, the tender infant of early age – women even in childbed have escaped violation, no sanctuary for protection avails, the barbarians in former ages respected the Altar, there was a secure refuge from violence for the tender and aged female, and for the ministers of the Altar, – but these modern barbarians have overthrown all obstacles, all governments and all religion wherever they have advanced.

> It behoves us therefore as Britons, as men who respect the Throne, who reverence our Religion, and the Constitution of England, to arm ...

It is difficult not to feel that Poole and his 'nest' of democrats may have served as a foil for all this high prose, and an excuse for the niagara of alcoholic toasts which went with it. *The heat was on.* You did not volunteer or not-volunteer, according to fancy. Every gentleman, every professional man, was under scrutiny. Moreover, even volunteering was not the end of the matter. The literary historian remembers May and June, 1798, for Hazlitt's idyllic visit to Stowey, his walk with Coleridge to Linton and Porlock Bay. The military historian, studying somewhat less entrancing records, remembers that in these months a new volunteer corps was founded 'for the Defence of the Coast, and adjacent country, from West Point to Porlock Bay.' 'I am happy to have it in my power to say,' the commander wrote to the Lord Lieutenant of Somerset:

> that Loyalty and the strongest Attachment to the excellent Constitution under which they live, seem to be Sensations nearest to the Heart of Each Individual. But notwithstanding the Conviction which I entertain of the Loyalty of those who have thus come forward, yet my Lord I hold it of the highest Importance to use every Means in my Power for investigating (as far as it is possible) the real State of every Man's Feelings, previous to his being entrusted with those Arms, which Government shall think proper to supply.

The poets, when they went to Germany, were hopping the draft.

This then is a part of the background to Coleridge's 'Fears in Solitude,' written in April, 1798. It is a poem of conflict, a drawing of the balance, but with an unmistakable conclusion, of reconciliation with 'O dear Britain, O my Mother Isle' – the church tower the four great elms of Stowey. But the oscillator was not likely to rest at that point for long, and the argument was going on among their friends as well. We get near to the conversations of the time from scraps of information in the diaries of James Losh. On March 24 he noted a conversation with a friend:

> who rises in my opinion – his steady opposition to a detestable

administration at home and to an insolent enemy from abroad agrees exactly with my opinion.

On April 3 he was talking with Southey:

> Our conversation turned principally upon the invasion of the liberty. I stated the probability of a stop being put to Southey's Joan of Arc, in that case he declared his intention of leaving this country. We all agreed that were there any place to go to emigration would be a prudent thing for literary men and the friends of freedom ...

In March, Wordsworth had been writing to Losh (of whom he was to see a good deal in the summer) expressing interest in his new journal, *The Oeconomist*. It was a quiet, indeed, a very safe, little journal, published in Newcastle. On the front was a block with a girl who represents truth, liberty, and virtue, seated with a cap of liberty beside her; in the background were rural implements, a ploughman, ships.

Losh was, in fact – as the entry in his diary at the end of 1798 shows – rapidly disengaging himself from political activism and was perhaps even one of those whom Coleridge had in mind when he wrote to Wordsworth in the summer of 1799 of those who 'in consequence of the complete failure of the French Revolution, have thrown up all hopes of the amelioration of mankind, and are sinking into an almost epicurean selfishness, disguising the same under the soft titles of domestic attachment and contempt for visionary *philosophes*.' But how are we to reconstruct Wordsworth's inner conflicts at this time? There is little evidence. The decision to withdraw to Germany was very sudden. On March 5, Dorothy wrote to Mary Huchinson to say that they had had a final refusal to renew the lease on Alfoxden: 'It is most probable that we shall go back again to Racedown.' On March 6, Wordsworth wrote to Tobin: 'I am at present utterly unable to say where we shall be.' On March 11, he was writing to

Losh: 'We have come to a resolution, Coleridge, Mrs. Coleridge, my Sister, and myself of going into Germany, where we purpose to pass the two ensuing years ...' Drummed out of the neighbourhood, they made the decision within a week. It was also a withdrawal from the vortex of an unbearable political conflict.

From the poetry we can learn much more. He has told us that his first great crisis came, not with the Revolution – this seemed to him in the course of 'nature' – nor with the Terror, but with the opening of hostilities between England and France in 1793:

> No shock
> Given to my moral nature had I known
> Down to that very moment ...

The shock was the greater in that he placed the blame upon his own government and nation:

> I felt
> The ravage of this most unnatural strife
> In my own heart; there lay it like a weight
> At enmity with all the tenderest springs
> Of my enjoyments. I, who with the breeze
> Had play'd, a green leaf on the blessed tree
> Of my beloved country; nor had wish'd
> For happier fortune than to wither there,
> Now from my pleasant station was cut off,
> And toss'd about in whirlwinds ...

It was not that he felt impelled to join his country against the new republic. It was rather the shock of the sense of alienation from his own people – from nature – which the predicament brought to him:

> This threw me first out of the pale of love;
> Sour'd and corrupted upwards to the source

> My sentiments, was not, as hitherto,
> A swallowing up of lesser things in great;
> But change of them into their opposites ...

It was this which had led him into Godwinism. We have seen how unbearable the continuing sense of alienation must have been to him at Alfoxden in 1797-1798. But Germany, momentarily outside the armed conflict, where he had hoped to find congenial intellectual and political company, did not alleviate this isolation. Leaving Coleridge to live in high style, on borrowed money (and with his puzzled and penniless wife and child at home), the Wordsworths travelled to Goslar before one of the hardest winters of the century clamped down upon them. They met no company. They had no money to entertain. There, in the utter isolation of self-exile, huddled by a stove in North Europe, he set to work on the *Prelude*. The unlovely Directory had given way to the brilliant Corsican general. The long war had lost its rationale as a war of republican defence:

> And now, become oppressors in their turn,
> Frenchmen had changed a war of self-defence
> For one of conquest, losing sight of all
> Which they had struggled for; and mounted up
> Openly, in the view of earth and heaven,
> The scale of Liberty ...

In Germany he found a disenchantment profounder than his own. The venerable Klopstock – a former honorary citizen of the Republic – upon whom they had waited on their first arrival, had relapsed into quietism. And for Wordsworth there were worse experiences to come. In the armed truce of 1802, the brief interval in that interminable war, he crossed the Channel to Calais to see Annette. There on the road where twelve years before he had seen 'banners, and happy faces, far and nigh':

> ... now, sole register that these things were,
> Two solitary greetings have I heard,
> 'Good morrow, Citizen!,' a hollow word,
> As if a dead man spake it. Yet despair
> Touches me not, though pensive as a bird
> Whose vernal coverts winter hath laid bare.

It is the same image of the leaf torn from the tree, but now he sees himself as precariously perched on the tree itself, exposed to the winds to come. Thousands of Englishmen, some of them, like Thomas Poole, former Jacobins, were pouring across the Channel to gape at republican France. But republican France had betrayed herself beyond redemption, in Wordsworth's eyes, by acclaiming a general as first consul for life. He voiced his uttermost contempt for the visitors, not because they visited the former enemy, but because they congratulated a France who had betrayed herself:

> Or what is it that ye go forth to see?
> Lords, lawyers, statesmen, squires of law degree ...

> When truth, when sense, when liberty were flown,
> What hardship had it been to wait an hour?

It is all there, in the great series of sonnets on independence and liberty. I cannot discuss them further. There were two twists of feeling, following close upon each other. The first, the resumption of war, but this time a war for which he felt France was responsible – an aggressor, and an imperialist aggressor. It was now England which appeared as 'the only light/Of Liberty that now remains on earth.' Thence flowed the patriotic sonnets, those curious medleys of rhetoric and controlled tension ('Oh grief that Earth's best hopes rest all with Thee!'), in which the long sense of alienation began to break down.

The second twist was the transference of his old affirmative humanist impulses to those moments of national resistance *against* the French – especially the Swiss resistance and the Spanish insurrection. Through these years, too, until 1805, he was writing the *Prelude*. It is easy enough to make fun of Wordsworth's apostasy, which was in some senses abject, in his last forty years. What is less easy is to conceive how he upheld, through all the preceding fifteen years, so great a confidence that 'fair seasons yet will come, and hopes as fair.' For one must look far in European literature to find any affirmation as proud as that with which he concluded the second book of the *Prelude*:

> ... if in these times of fear,
> This melancholy waste of hopes o'erthrown,
> If, 'mid indifference and apathy
> And wicked exultation, when good men,
> On every side fall off we know not how,
> To selfishness, disguis'd in gentle names
> Of peace, and quiet, and domestic love,
> Yet mingled, not unwillingly, with sneers
> On visionary minds; if in this time
> Of dereliction and dismay, I yet
> Despair not of our nature; but retain
> A more than Roman confidence, a faith
> That fails not, in all sorrow my support,
>
> The blessing of my life, the gift is yours,
> Ye mountains! thine, O Nature!

* * *

I recalled that in 1956 or 1957, when John Gates, then editor of the American *Daily Worker*, resigned from the Communist Party after the crisis arising from the Hungarian rising, he was reported in the press as saying: 'I am not leaving anything, I am rejoining the American people.'

It is a phrase which stayed in my mind. On one hand, the movement of feeling can be understood. Is it not comparable in some ways to that of 1803? Isolated for so long from the 'national consensus,' the target for unremitting attack, in defence of a cause which they increasingly doubted at heart, this moment must have appeared like a rejoining, a cutting of an unbearable tension.

But on the other hand, the phrase had something ugly about it, some taste of the apostate. Mr. Gates may be at this day a man of independent judgment who has not affected a wholesale repudiation of his past. But one recalls that there have been so many others, in whom a 'rejoining' has been accompanied by a giving up of the problem – a caricaturing of themselves – even a shrugging off of personal responsibilities for difficult problems and errors by attributing them to some outside element, some set of principles or party, some 'Naked God' or 'God that Failed.' And the psychology of apostasy is more complex than that. There is that peculiar and vengeful kind of bitterness which a certain kind of man finds for an idealized mistress who has disappointed him.

I introduce these wholly irrelevant reflections because I have often pondered what rejoining the British people, in 1798 or 1803, was like. It was, after all, not only an England engaged in a war of national defence; it was also an England suppressing Irish rebellion with a ferocity which outdistances the French Terror: an England of soaring bread prices and near starvation. It meant rejoining the nation of the *Anti-Jacobin Review*. For Thomas Poole, it meant serving in the Volunteers alongside those gentry who had, five years before, seen Wordsworth out of the country and hedged around the marvellous tanner himself with alcoholic rhetoric and espionage. It meant submitting to the vastly complacent 'I told you so' of the smug Church and King patriots, like Justice Bolt in Crabbe's tale 'The Dumb Orators' – Justice Bolt, who:

... seated with his former air,
Look'd his full self, and fill'd his ample chair.
Took one full bumper to each favourite cause,
And dwelt all night on politics and laws,
With high applauding voice, that gain'd him high applause.

I must argue that capitulation by the Jacobin poets to the traditional, paternalistic culture was in fact inimical to the sources of their art. It was not inimical right through the intellectual spectrum. Some of Coleridge's great criticism belongs to the years of apostasy. (Perhaps the pages of the *Partisan Review* and of *Dissent,* and the careers of several now famous contributors, might confirm that some measure of apostasy, some defection from cultural affirmatives, has proved to be, in our time also, a stimulant to the critical faculties?) But there was, in the early 1800s, a sad sense of a narrowing of sympathies, a contraction of the heart, a burning down of the fires, in all that circle. Mr. Poole emerged in the Volunteers as a good bourgeois, a *useful* man. He experienced some ill turn from his servants, and learned from it, instantly, a bourgeois moral. The context of his letter to Coleridge suggests that the ill turn may perhaps have been some betrayal of personal confidences:

> Now this is a proof of such melancholy insensibility on their part, not to say depravity, and so damps every benevolent feeling of my own mind, as far as relates to their class of society, that it is difficult to say how injurious to me, and to them, the consequences of it may be ...thus, my dear Col., we must look to ourselves, and I am afraid to ourselves alone, for happiness. Woe be to him who cannot in these days turn with satisfaction from the contemplation of the species to the contemplation of himself – who cannot keep the little court of his own breast swept clean of the degrading passions and low vices ...

64

Coleridge was only too ready to return the sympathy for which the former Jacobin had asked:

> As to your servants and the people of Stowey in general, Poole, my beloved! You have been often unwisely fretful with me when I have pressed upon you their depravity. Without religious joys and religious terrors, nothing can be expected from the *inferior* classes in society ...

We are a long way from the Family of Love. We are very close to Fathers and Mothers of the Victorians. These disappointed men were being driven back upon themselves – the contemplation *of* themselves. Coleridge was increasingly self-preoccupied, hypochondriacal, petulant about money, addicted. The egotism of Wordsworth enlarged, but fortunately it enlarged first of all within poetic autobiography. We have passed out of the Alfoxden summer and into that autumn of the Lakes which De Quincey was to describe, in a book which, read in one way, is to be recommended only as the most catty book in our literature, but which, read in another way, is a work of lyrical melancholy.

Nor is this self-contemplation unrelated to the poetic *détente* of Wordsworth. How far is it possible for men to hold on to aspirations long after there appears to be no hope of inserting them into 'the real world which is the world of all of us'? If the social context makes all insertion seem impossible – if all objective referents for these hopes are cruelly obliterated – if the attempt to live out the ideals appears to produce their opposite – if *fraternité* produces fratricide, *égalité* produces empire, liberty produces liberticide – then aspirations can only become a transposed interior faith. There may be a deepening of sensibility. But the dangers are also evident. This driving back into interior faith, this preoccupation with trying to 'hold' and to meditate upon past states of feeling, is surely the clue not only to the increasingly self-preoccupied tone of Wordsworth's life, and style of life, as the Lake Poet, but also to the increasing failure of *observation* even in his nature poetry. The new Wordsworth was becoming (despite large philosophic apostrophes) less responsive to nature, more obsessed with the loss of inspiration. As one moves beyond 1805, one recalls those lines from 'The Ruined Cottage,' which might have passed a prophetic comment upon the sources of his own inspiration:

> The Waters of that spring if they could feel
> Might mourn. They are not as they were, the bond
> Of brotherhood is broken; time has been
> When every day the touch of human hand
> Disturbed their stillness, and they ministered
> To human comfort ...

This setting back can be seen throughout the *Excursion*. Professor Hough has written of this poem that it 'is one of the great reassertions of traditional values against the unhistorical rationalist optimism of the enlightenment.' This is true, but one must also add 'alas!' In the tension between these areas Wordsworth had found great poetry; in the relapse he simply wrote down his own genius. As he revised 'The Ruined Cottage,' so the old paternalistic tag-words drop back in: 'rosy' children, 'homely' fare, 'the keen, the wholesome, air of poverty.' Margaret's 'husband' ('an industrious man Sober and steady') becomes 'her wedded Partner.' The Wanderer commences as a self-taught Cumbrian shepherd boy, fond of the songs of Burns; he ends as a literary product of the Scottish kirk. The Jacobin solitary is there, to be sure, and at moments the real tension of his disenchantment flares into life. But he is, for the most part, a philosophical clay model for pins. He has been beaten by every accident of life, beset by domestic tragedy, political defeat, philosophical bankruptcy. He can scarcely answer back as pedlar, poet, and parson all set about him. As Wordsworth wrote to Sir George Beaumont, he was at work on the poem, 'I hope tolerably well, and certainly with good views.'

So Wordsworth fell back within the forms of paternalistic sensibility. If there is a moral, it is not that he became a poorer poet because he changed his political views, but that his new 'good views' were not held with the same intensity and authenticity. They are too dutiful, too much the product not of the poet but of his inner moral censor; he wrote, not out of belief, nor out of the tension between beliefs, but out of a sense of what he *ought* to believe. Good views seldom make good poetry, whether these views are those approved of by the Anglican Church or the vanguard of the working class.

If I speak of apostasy, then, it is one way of saying that in area after area the poets fell back within the traditional frame of paternalism, Anglican doctrine, fear of change. It would be dismal to go over the record. There were moments when the poets were ludicrous or contemptible. After the wars, the revival of a vigorous plebeian democratic movement at home inflamed all their fears of revolution and yet drew forth no response. There was Southey (then poet laureate), who attempted to secure an injunction in the high courts against the pirating of his own 'Wat Tyler.' There was Coleridge, author of 'Conciones,' now demanding the shackling of the radical press (to which Wordsworth reluctantly assented) and addressing his 'Lay Sermon' to the higher and middle classes (1817) in language which had patently passed beyond his control: the 'fetid flower' – 'the incendiary and his kindling combustibles' – 'These noisy and calumnious zealots, whom ...St. John beheld in the Apocalyptic vision as a compound of locust and scorpion ...are the perennials of history.' There was, most lamentable of all, Wordsworth actively supporting the Lowther interest in his own Lakeland against the independent statesmen, resisting reform as obstinately as the old Duke himself, and declaring:

> I cannot but be of opinion that the feudal power yet surviving
> in England is eminently serviceable in counteracting the
> popular tendency to reform ...The people are already powerful
> far beyond the increase of their information and their
> improvement in morals.

There came the moment when Wordsworth simply gave
up. In 1809 he could still write the 'Tract on the Convention of
Cintra': but after 1815 he wrote no tract on the Congress of
Vienna, when Old Legitimacy was reestablished on the
thrones of Europe. And there was that stealthy reconciliation
to the establishment – the patronage of the Lonsdales – the
convenient manner (described with such heavy irony by De
Quincey) in which his material needs were attended to. All this
may be resumed in one instance – if we recall what we are
saying, all the history that seems to be rewritten – when we
know that Wordsworth and Coleridge entered into social
exchanges with the greatest luminary of Lake Society: Richard
Watson, Bishop of Llandaff.

I have tried to distinguish between apostasy, a relapse into
received patterns of thought and feeling, often accompanied by
self-mutilation and the immoderate reverse of attachments,
and disenchantment. I cannot think that disenchantment is at
enmity with poetry; one might as well suppose that honesty is
so. I wish sometimes that Shelley's verse had been stiffened
with a touch of it, that he had written an ode to the east wind.

Again, I see little point in abusing the poets for their later
apostasy. How long could any man have stood a tension of that
sort, at its full creative intensity, between a vision of the
universal heart, and the marching and countermarching of
armies across Europe? There must be *some* objective referent
for social hope, and it is one trick of the mind to latch on to an
unworthy object in order to sustain such hope. Those who did

not become apostates in this circle did not fare much better. Some, like James Losh, became cautious Whigs and exponents of the new political economy, whose cash equivalents opened up a distance between men immeasurably colder than that of Tory paternalism. Hazlitt preserved much of the early vision, and burst out when the *Excursion* was published:

> All things move, not in progress, but in a ceaseless round; our strength lies in our weakness; our virtues are built on our vices; our faculties are as limited as our being; nor can we lift man above his nature more than above the earth he treads. But though we cannot weave over again the airy, unsubstantial dream, which reason and experience have dispelled ...yet we will never cease, nor be prevented from returning on the wings of imagination to that bright dream of our youth; that glad dawn of the day-star of liberty; that spring-time of the world, in which the hopes and expectations of the human race seemed opening in the same gay career with our own; when France called her children to partake her equal blessings beneath her laughing skies; when the stranger was met in all her villages with dance and festive songs; in celebration of a new and golden era ...The dawn of that day was suddenly overcast; that season of hope is past; it is fled with the other dreams of our youth, which we cannot recall, but has left behind it traces, which are not to be effaced by Birthday and Thanks-giving Odes, or the chanting of *Te Deums* in all the churches of Christendom. To those hopes eternal regrets are due: to those who maliciously and wilfully blasted them, in the fear that they might be accomplished, we feel no less what we owe – hatred and scorn as lasting!

But there is a curious arrest, a stasis, in this: the passage works by means of a tension between stale libertarian rhetoric ('glad dawn,' 'day-star,' 'golden era') pressed to the point of self-mockery, nostalgic rhythms, and sudden, muscular polemic. Hazlitt could maintain his affirmatives only by latching on to the hero figure of Napoleon, and by sustaining his aspiration of a kind of whimsy fortified by rancor.

It is obvious enough that there is, within this history, some parallel with our own times. This is one of the fascinations of the period. And one of its dangers. The glib comparisons rise up, and they lie beneath the surface even when unstated. The French and the Russian revolutions; the Coalitions and N.A.T.O.; the Spanish insurrection and Hungary, 1956; Godwinism and Marxism. Scrupulously examined, most of these comparisons break down, but as a more general matter of historical *process*, of revolution and reaction, of divided loyalties, of universal visions and limiting realities, of commitment and disenchantment, the parallels remain.

The large political affirmatives of humanism took a tremendous beating during those years, and they have taken another beating in our own half-century. In some ways they took a greater beating in English culture than in French. In France, the Revolution, when all the dust had settled, left great residual achievements. Moreover, the cause of the Revolution had become entwined with that of national pride. French historians have, perhaps, never fully appreciated the traumatic consequences upon international Jacobinism of the Revolution's defection from its own egalitarian principles: one thinks of Wordsworth at Calais, lamenting the imprisonment of Citizen Toussaint, the reinstatement of slavery in the French West Indies.

In the France of the 1820s Julien Sorel could gaze upon the portrait of Napoleon as emblematic of the meteoric rise of obscure talent. But in England the Revolution brought little but the defeat of one of the most generous impulses in our culture. It opened no career to talents save that of the apostate. Not one of its watchwords – fraternity or liberty or *égalité* – was advanced on British soil. All appeared, within the eye of a culture presided over by military anti-Jacobins, as discredited.

And this was accompanied by the autosuppression of these aspirations within the breasts of those who had first espoused them.

Hence, in Britain, the 1790s have remained shrouded in guilt and obscurity until the present day. What was left, rather, was a well worn path within our culture – what might be called 'the Bishop of Llandaff's Slide' – from humanist love to old obscurantist accommodation. Peacock, in *Nightmare Abbey*, shows us Flosky (or Coleridge) at the bottom of this slide:

> He had been in his youth an enthusiast for liberty and he had hailed the dawn of the French Revolution as the promise of a day that was to banish war and slavery, and every form of vice and misery from the face of the earth. Because all this was not done, he deduced that nothing was done: and ...from this deduction, according to his system of logic, he drew a conclusion that worse than nothing was done: that the overthrow of the feudal fortresses of tyranny and superstition was the greatest calamity that had ever befallen mankind; and that their only hope now was to rake the rubbish together, and rebuild it without any of those loopholes by which the light had originally crept in ...

Ever since this time, the stations of the slide, the ritual gestures, have all formed a cultural pattern into which, with the least encouragement, the novitiate might enter. This prepared the way for that precipitate disavowal of their past, by the leftist generation of the thirties, which C. Wright Mills, in a late lecture, described as 'cultural default.' And it is this fault in our culture which helps us to understand the rapidity with which, in our own time, poets have been able to pass from callow affirmations to even more callow repudiations of politics and the world. It has even been possible to enter station 2 or 3 of the slide – the stations of utter disenchantment – without having to go through the tedium and intellectual vulgarity of a prior enchantment.

But this is surely to miss, somewhere, the point. I am reminded of this, most forcibly, when I notice the use to which Mary Wollstonecraft is put in some recent psychological and sociological writing. How convenient it is that this most rational of women, who proclaimed the equality of sexes and who attempted to live her principles in free marriage, should have been driven to attempted suicide by an unhappy love affair, and then should have died in childbirth – a death (as the *Anti-Jacobin Review* was quick to point out) 'that strongly marked the distinction of the sexes' and 'pointed out the destiny of woman.' How neat an ornament she provided for the anti-Jacobin moralist: 'A woman, who had broken through all religious restraints, will, commonly, be found ripe for every species of licentiousness.' But the moral, if in language somewhat more quaint, has been repeated ever since. I find in a work entitled Modern Woman – the Lost Sex, which has had a considerable spell of influence in the United States, that Mary provides a case history throughout, to illustrate that women who fret against their sociological roles have got it coming to them. She was, it seems, 'afflicted with a severe case of penis-envy ...The facts of Mary Wollstonecraft's life show [that] the shadow of the phallus lay darkly, threateningly, over every move she made.'

It does not occur to these moralists that Mary Wollstonecraft was a casualty, and to my mind an heroic casualty, of transition, and that all great transitions, in social or in personal relations, must have their casualty lists. Too large an appetite for human perfectibility may be folly; but I like the other end of the Bishop's slide rather less. I cannot see the 1790s, with their overfacile faith in *fraternité* and *égalité*, as no more than a museum for the moralists. And I think most often of Wordsworth, isolated in Goslar in the winter of 1799, 'this melancholy waste of hopes o'erthrown,' 'when good men/ On every side fall off, we know not how,' pitting himself against all inclination to thresh the grain of humanism from the chaff. Without the 1790s there would have been no harvest to thresh.

It is not the apostate point of rest that is worth our attention, but the conflict along the way, out of which the great art sprang. I could wish that Mr. Auden could have shown some part of that Roman confidence, when he came to the same place of conflict in September, 1939. In our time, men have been disenchanted too easily, in too much hurry to pass through to the station of apostasy. But I will end with some lines from one American poet, Thomas McGrath, who has remained a doubting Jacobin for twenty years in the heart of the New Legitimacy, and who has still not taken to the Bishop's slide:

> It is the charm which the potential has
> That is the proper aura for the poem ...
>
> Though every battle, every augury,
> Argue defeat, and if defeat itself
> Bring all the darkness level with our eyes -
> It is the poem provides the proper charm
> Spelling resistance and the living will,
> To bring to dance a stony field of fact
> And set against terror exile or despair
> The rituals of our humanity.

NOTES

I am also indebted to the librarians and staff of the following institutions for their assistance and for permission to cite passages from unpublished papers: Dr. Williams' Library (Henry Crabb Robinson correspondence); the Houghton Library, Harvard University (John Thelwall to Dr. Crompton, 1798); the Pierpont Morgan Library (John Thelwall to Mrs. Thelwall, 1798); the British Museum (Cumberland

THE ROMANTICS

MSS); Tullie House, Carlisle (Diary of James Losh); and the Public
Record Office, London (Treasury Solicitor's Papers, Home Office
Papers; I am indebted to Mr. Malcolm Thomas, of the University of
Warwick, for directing my attention to the papers of the Somerset
Volunteers in the latter source).

WORDSWORTH'S CRISIS

'I am of that odious class of men called democrats,' Wordsworth wrote to his friend William Mathews in 1794. Much the same can be said of Coleridge, on the evidence of his letters and publications of the mid-1790s. By the early decades of this century, British, French and American scholarship concurred in finding both poets to be, in the 1790s, republicans and advanced reformers, who then suffered disappointment in the course of the French Revolution and, in different ways and at different times, changed their minds. George McLean Harper's *William Wordsworth: His Life, Works and Influence* (1919) set a coping-stone on the scholarship of that period.

In subsequent decades, despite much patient editorial scholarship, the matter of the poets' 'revolutionary' youth has been obscured and marginalised. A new study was needed, consolidating and reviewing the evidence, and this is what Nicholas Roe offers. He claims no startling discoveries, but he brings together in one place much scattered information and a few new details from Godwin's papers. His treatment of the tradition of Dissent in Cambridge fills out what Schneider, Chard and others have already shown. His treatment of London Godwinian and 'Jacobin' circles draws upon sources which literary scholars often ignore. Wordsworth and Coleridge are replaced within a credible human context, in the midst of a like-minded radical intelligentsia: William Frend, George Dyer, John Thelwall, Basil Montagu, John Tweddell, Felix Vaughan, James Losh, Joseph Fawcett.

Roe's research has been strenuous, his attention to detail earnest, and his book will be useful. But it will not be quite as useful as the book which he intended to write, which would have brought poetic text and historical context into dialogue with each other. In this he succeeds best in his fourth chapter, which examines the genesis and transformation of poetry of 'social protest' between 1793 and 1798. There he was able to take advantage of work already done: by Gill on 'Salisbury Plain', by Butler on 'The Ruined Cottage', by Jacobus, Jonathan Wordsworth and others.

Elsewhere he is less successful. His history is more literary-biographical than intellectual, and he passes by without comment significant work in intellectual history. James Chandler's Wordsworth's Second Nature (1984) goes unmentioned, and Chandler's and Roe's Wordsworths might be two different people. Were I forced to choose between them I would opt for Roe's. I remain unconvinced by Chandler's catch-all use of Burke and by his attribution of influences from Le Moniteur: that is too academic a portrait of how Wordsworth put together his ideas. Like many poets and like most lay-persons, Wordsworth (I suspect) grabbed ideas half-formed out of the discourse of his social environment and rarely read a work of political theory from end to end. (He would not pursue his reading of the second edition of Godwin's Political Justice because he found the preface to be 'a piece of barbarous writing'.) Yet Chandler's arguments are open and challenging where Roe is sometimes anecdotal and even anti-intellectual. Rousseau's work goes unmentioned, and while Godwin is mentioned frequently there is little attention to Godwin's ideas, nor to the reasons why the poets were both attracted and repelled by them. Roe's Wordsworth is not intellectual enough.

There was something secretive about Wordsworth through much of the 1790s, and secretive in more than the matter of Annette Vallon (which was so successfully hushed up). It must follow that any biographer must engage in speculations. But Roe offers too many speculations of this order: 'As Wordsworth parted from Losh in July 1797 it seems highly likely that politics, poetry, his recent past and immediate future would have been in his mind.' Yes, and perhaps also the score at the Nag's Head which Losh had left him to settle? At times he seems even to prefer speculations to actual findings. Thus he speculates that an anonymous review ('The Matter of Coleridge's Revolutionary Youth', *TLS*, 6 August 1971) might have been written by E.P. Thompson, a speculation which could have been translated into a finding at the cost of a postage stamp. But his speculations do not always compel assent. Thus his book is illustrated by a Gillray cartoon of a London Corresponding Society open-air meeting, and in the caption we are informed that an obscure blob behind one speaker is 'Citizen' Wordsworth sitting in a tree. Why on earth should Gillray have taken notice of Wordsworth in 1795? (Perhaps Roe is pulling our leg?) On other occasions he introduces confusion by mingling together real findings and false conclusions. Thus he finds that two of the associates of the poets, James Losh and William Frend, were members of a committee concerned with raising funds for the defendants after the 1794 treason trials. This is of interest, but it is then translated into the untrue statement that 'there was a very considerable Cambridge element among the leadership of the Corresponding Society.' As attention to Mary Thale's comprehensive and scrupulously-edited Selections from the Papers of the LCS makes clear, none of the supposed Cambridge element served on the Society's executive or general committees, and it is doubtful whether any were ever members.

It is a borderline situation, perhaps not worth labouring. Of the poets' known acquaintance, only John Thelwall was, off and on, a member (and *de facto* a leader) of the LCS. George Dyer contributed to the Society's *Moral and Political Magazine* in 1796, and helped to raise funds for victims of persecution. Felix Vaughan appears more often in the Society's Minutes, but in his capacity as a (generous) barrister, defending political victims. Frend, whom Roe several times claims as a 'leader' of the LCS, was probably never a member of the Society, but he did share the LCS platform in the final climactic public protest against the Two Acts in December 1795, and in that sense – as part of an alliance which stretched from Charles James Fox through the genteel supporters of the Society for Constitutional Information to the largely shopkeeper and artisan LCS – he did perform a leading role. With a scrupulous sense of this borderline distinction, Francis Place noted down Frend as 'Mr' but the other speakers as 'Citizens'.

The SCI was intimidated by the treason trials and it scarcely resumed activity thereafter. When Wordsworth came to London early in 1795 there was no obvious reforming club or society for him to join. With few exceptions intellectuals or 'gentlemen' did not join the LCS. This was, no doubt, partly for reasons of social class, partly from a desire to hold themselves at a distance from the blunt Paineite or 'Jacobinical' discourse, and partly from a characteristic intellectual distaste for being committed to majority decisions or courses of action. But it is not impossible that Wordsworth and his friends might have visited divisions of the Society. In 1795, intellectual radicalism and the popular societies were bumping against each other all the time, and Nicholas Roe, if wrong in a few details, is right to bring them into such close juxtaposition.

Where Roe, in common with all researchers, becomes

puzzled is in the matter of the *Philanthropist*. In 1794 Wordsworth (then in the North) was writing to his friend, William Mathews, drawing up proposals for their conduct of a magazine with this name, to be commenced when Wordsworth could get to London. Roe discusses these plans with great seriousness, as if they had indeed been fulfilled. He even deduces from them that Wordsworth in 1794 was already a convert to Godwin: 'the *Philanthropist* scheme also provides clear evidence of William Godwin's influence in reference to 'Hereditary distinctions and privileged orders ...which must necessarily counteract the progress of human improvement'.' But, apart from the elevated tone, that is plain Tom Paine talk, to be found in any reform publication of the time. Then Roe tells the reader, some thirty pages on, that the scheme for the *Philanthropist* was 'never realised'. Wordsworth, writing to Mathews on 7 November 1794, had agreed that they must 'decline the field', since he was delayed in Keswick attending on his dying friend, Raisley Calvert. So there was no magazine. But then, in March 1795, shortly after Wordsworth had at last got to London, a *Philanthropist* does appear. This is a coincidence too large to pass off in a little cough in a footnote, although that is what scholars have generally done. Roe attends to it in an appendix, speculating upon possible contributors and reaching the cautious conclusion that Wordsworth 'may well have contributed in some capacity'.

I think that on this occasion his speculations might have been more bold. The journal is ill-edited and lazily conducted. It is an eight-page sheet, coming from the press of Daniel Isaac Eaton, a printer of great audacity who was repeatedly tried for sedition. Scholars have assumed that a Great Poet could have had no hand in such a sheet. Mrs Moorman assures us that 'it was scurrilous in style and contained nothing which could have issued from the pen of Wordsworth.'

I have in this matter one advantage over the majority

of literary scholars. I have myself been involved in editing oppositional publications, immersed among beautiful and ineffectual utopians and hissing factionalists, and I know that substantial miscellanies (such as Wordsworth and Mathews proposed) are not conjured out of air. They require ready contributors and a constituency of readers; finance; proficiency in organisation and editorial application. If we put together what we know of Wordsworth in 1795, we have no reason to suppose that he would succeed as a radical editor. *The Monthly Magazine* and the *Analytical Review* already occupied the ground of liberal miscellanies. Wordsworth had no money to spare and Mathews had less. He had no experience in editing and few contacts with contributors. We know from his (unpublished) 'Letter to the Bishop of Llandaff' that he could write in high-minded prose; and we know that he disliked the idea of taking on any regular journalistic chores (such as Parliamentary reporting) because that kind of thing gave him headaches. Any miscellany conducted by Wordsworth would have been short-lived.

The *Philanthropist* matches such expectations. It starts out sententiously, with each number given over to an essay in political morality. It later declines into a casually-edited collection of reprints and of satirical verses. The politics of the journal are constitutionalist-radical. The occasional Latin tag and the deference to Fox suggest the appeal to a polite rather than a popular audience. Several numbers are taken up with reprinting such matters as the Address to the Public of the Society for Constitutional Information in 1780, and John Trenchard's tract against standing armies.

I agree with Roe that the journal contains several passages which could have come from Wordsworth's pen. I would go further and suggest that Wordsworth may have been editorially involved. There are little signals which suggest some editorial confusion. The first number (16 March 1795) carries on its masthead: 'Printed for and sold by DANIEL ISAAC EATON, Printer and Bookseller to the Supreme Majesty of the People, at the COCK and SWINE, No 74, Newgate Street'. But the third and fourth numbers (30 March and 6 April) carry on their last page a pointing finger and the advice: 'Those who wish to promote the PHILANTHROPIST, by their assistance, will please address their favours to the Editors, at Mr EATON'S ...' There is then an unexplained gap of three weeks and when the journal resumes on 27 April the plural 'editors' has become the singular 'editor'. (Eaton's previous journal, *Politics for the People*, had never suggested such a division of editorial and publishing roles.) This is repeated from time to time until No 22 (Monday, 24 August). Thereafter all reference to an editor is dropped. One notes another coincidence: Wordsworth left London precipitately on or about 18 August on his way to Racedown.

If one were to invent a story which was to fit these signals and coincidences, it might run like this ...Wordsworth comes to London in late February and gets together with Mathews. They find that they have little money and they also find that printers eager to issue odious democratic journals are not to be found on every street. They go and see Citizen Eaton, whose shop is in any case an obvious meeting-point for reformers. Eaton had, on 25 January, published the last number of *Politics for the People*, so there was perhaps some underemployment of his press. He takes Wordsworth and Mathews's idea on, but talks them into scaling down their operation to a modest eight-page weekly. The partnership between the two editors survives for only four numbers, there is some collapse or quarrel, and then only one of them resumes. But the editor is increasingly inattentive or otherwise preoccupied, and Eaton has to fill up the pages with reprinted materials. Eventually (after Wordsworth left London) he conducts it himself. The *Philanthropist* continued until the

42nd number (18 January 1796), when, in the aftermath of the Two Acts, it was discontinued.

The *Philanthropist* was not so much 'scurrilous' as boring, and even if Wordsworth's association with it could be proved it would not add to his stature. One of the more interesting essays – 'On the Influence of Some Human Institutions on Human Happiness', signed 'W' – I once thought could be Wordsworth's and Roe suggests could be William Frend's. But it turns out to have been lifted from a more lively Norwich journal, the *Cabinet*. Several manuscript keys survive to the *Cabinet*'s anonymous contributors, and in two of these 'W' is identified as a Dr Rigby. One might plead, of course, that the compiler of these keys guessed wrongly, or that Dr Rigby was the 'front' through which a secretive Wordsworth passed his manuscript to the editor. The doctor was, in one reminiscence, 'a thorough-going Democrat of the French type, and in his country house a few miles from Norwich he had a Tree of Liberty around which his political confrères ...used to dance and sing the Marseillaise.' But no reminiscence shows Wordsworth or Coleridge among the dancers, so there, for the time being, the trail runs out.

If Wordsworth had anything to do with the *Philanthropist*, he hid his name behind Eaton's. Very little is known of that six months in London, apart from a few entries in Godwin's diary which do no more than record calls and callers. One is tempted to probe this darkness because there is the suggestion in the poet's subsequent writing that some profound moral crisis was associated with the Godwinian enchantment. Most critics find this in 'The Borderers' and also in the *Prelude* and *Excursion*. The crisis is associated less with 'France' than with 'false philosophy' in its bearing upon both public life and personal relations. One is tempted to speculate whether – just as the matter of Annette Vallon was covered up for a hundred years – there might not also be some political crisis or scandal hidden behind the verse?

In both the Prelude and Excursion this crisis is associated less with political commitment than with a retreat, in the aftermath of political disappointment and defeat, from immediate commitment to 'wild theories' and 'abstraction'. In the *Prelude*, it was

> when events
> Brought less encouragement, and unto these
> The immediate proof of principles no more
> Could be entrusted, while the events themselves,
> Worn out in greatness, and in novelty,
> Less occupied the mind

- it was then that 'evidence/Safer, of universal application' was sought elsewhere. There follows, after a reference to the French Republic's new aggressiveness, the passage which is rightly identified with the Godwinian enchantment:

> This was the time when all things tending fast
> To depravation, the Philosophy
> That promised to abstract the hopes of man
> Out of his feelings, to be fix'd thenceforth
> For ever in a purer element
> Found ready welcome.

And after sixty or more lines of accusation and of self-accusation Wordsworth turns away with the suggestion of something still unrevealed:

> Time may come
> When some dramatic Story may afford
> Shapes livelier to convey to thee, my Friend,
> What then I learn'd, or think I learn'd, of truth,
> And the errors into which I was betray'd ...

This 'dramatic Story' perhaps came in the *Excursion*, in

the figure of the Solitary, lampooned as a Janus-faced hypocrite, who in 'private life licentiously displayed/Unhallowed actions' and who in public drew

> Hopeful prognostications from a creed,
> That, in the light of false philosophy,
> Spread like a halo round a misty moon,
> Widening its circle as the storms advance.

And in the Solitary's own account (or self-flagellation?) the same sequence is suggested. It was when the revolutionary cause encountered complexities and defeats and 'confusion reigned' that the Solitary espoused more extreme doctrines. The passage is at Book Three, line 768, and concludes (787):

> Among men
> So charactered did I maintain a strife
> Hopeless, and still more hopeless every hour;
> But, in the process, I began to feel
> That, if the emancipation of the world
> Were missed, I should at least secure my own,
> And be in part compensated. For rights,
> Widely – inveterately usurped upon,
> I spake with vehemence; and promptly seized
> All that Abstraction furnished for my needs
> Or purposes; nor scrupled to proclaim,
> And propagate, by liberty of life,
> Those new persuasions ...

In Roe's work what is missing is any clear view of a climactic crisis with 'false philosophy', giving rise to a flight from its temptations and to a decade of arduous self-reflection. As Roe struggles through a thick undergrowth of associates and of speculations, no clear path of analysis is laid open. He has some helpful pages where he shows the ambiguity of both poets in their feelings towards Robespierre. This contributed to a crisis, which, however – if we are to follow the hints in the *Prelude* and Excursion - came about, not in terms of French politics, but in terms of English thought. Roe insists, on slender grounds, upon pre-dating Wordsworth's enchantment with Godwinism to 1793-4, and as for his disenchantment this is attributed to nothing more dramatic than commonplace disillusion when he came to London and met his guru in the flesh. Godwin's conversation was long-winded and dogmatic, and Roe suggests that Wordsworth's ' "sage" turned out to be a nit-picking pedant'. The explanation seems inadequate.

A poet's internal crises may take place in private regions which biographers cannot reach. There need be no evident objective referents for tumults of the spirit. But if Roe had probed more closely into his own contexts, alternative explanations might have arisen. 1795 was the *annus mirabilis* of advanced intellectual radicalism, which moved in different ways and according to different rhythms from the popular societies. This was the time, which Hazlitt was to recall, when 'the doctrine of Universal Benevolence, the belief in the Omnipotence of Truth and in the Perfectibility of Human Nature', 'were spoken on the house-tops, were whispered in secret, were published in quarto and duodecimo, in political treatises, in plays, poems, songs and romances – made their way to the bar, crept into the church, ascended the rostrum, thinned the classes of the universities ...' When Burke fulminated against '80,000 incorrigible Jacobins' he was thinking not of the popular societies but of the young radical intelligentsia of Britain. These were the students, young attorneys, merchants' sons and daughters, who signalled their advanced views by changes in dress and hair-style, in education and child care and breast-feeding, in pedestrian excursions – even genteel women could now get about the countryside, as Dorothy Wordsworth did, provided that they could find some boots. Here were the analogues of the notaries and curés of France, with their resentment at interest and patronage and their demand for the career open to talent. 1795, in the aftermath of the acquittals in the treason trials and before the passing of the Two Acts, was a brief moment of 'glasnost', when debating clubs for the enlightened intelligentsia sprang up: the Philomathaeans, where Roe has found Godwin, Holcroft and John Binns of the LCS, and Tusculan School which supplied contributors to the *Cabinet*, women's discussion clubs in Norwich, Belfast and perhaps elsewhere.

This was the milieu in which *Political Justice* (and also the *Rights of Woman*) found enthusiastic audience. The tone (or cant) of the time is exemplified by a contribution concerning spies and informers in the *Cabinet*: 'Whoever has been accustomed to reason abstractedly, on the moral estimation in which particular classes of men should be held, or on the advantages attending political institutions, and to deduce his principles from arguments, drawn *a priori* from the nature of man, and who at the same time has surveyed men with attention, will probably feel a diversity of opinion, according to the different *media* through which he examines the objects of his attention.' One might not conclude, from this elevated passage, that the author was an articled attorney in his 20th year, Henry Crabb Robinson. Nor did Wordsworth in the *Prelude* ridicule the aspirations of the Rule of Benevolence and Reason – 'a noble aspiration, yet I feel/The aspiration:

> the dream
> Was flattering to the young ingenuous mind
> Pleas'd with extremes, and not the least with that
> Which makes the human Reason's naked self
> The object of its fervour.

In retrospect, Robinson still affirmed that reading *Political Justice* 'made me feel more generously. I had never felt before, nor, I am afraid, have I ever since felt so strongly, the duty of not living to oneself, but of having for one's sole object the good of the community.' His private correspondence illustrates his Godwinian infatuation. Late in 1797, he was writing to his brother to congratulate him on the birth of a son, while not neglecting to warn him against the trap of 'natural affections': '*Our* Philosophy has freed us from a weighty pack of instincts & natural affections which antient philosophers have stuck upon the human frame & constitution like burrs & patches.' And, in a discussion of marriage, he wrote: 'You deprecate the progress of that philosophy which tends to diminish the individual & exclusive attachment. But the utmost asserted by Godwin or any of the new Philosophers ...is that our attachments should be regulated only by the moral & intellectual worth of the object regardless of the *accidents* of birth, early acquaintance, &c &c.' This is the same Godwin as that recalled by Hazlitt, who 'absolves man from the gross and narrow ties of sense, custom, authority, private and local attachment, in order that he may devote himself to the boundless pursuit of universal benevolence'.

To the historian of ideas Godwinism may appear as the *ne plus ultra* of advanced democratic thought in the 1790s. After plain Tom Paineism (1791-1794) the new wave of Godwin seems to have engulfed most advanced radical intellectuals between 1794 and 1797. Wordsworth by his own confession was engulfed. 'Throw aside your books of chemistry,' he is said to have advised a student in the Temple, 'and read Godwin on Necessity.' Coleridge with his usual ambivalence was attracted and repelled; wrote a sonnet in praise of Godwin and said he had never read him; denounced him offensively in public and apologised to him in private; had it down in his notebook to do a root-and-branch critique which never, of course, was done.

But the actual record was not so simple. Not one of the men who acquired notoriety as public reformers, as active opponents of government, as advocates of peace, friends of France, or supporters of the popular reform societies, was a Godwinian. William Frend and Gilbert Wakefield were advanced Unitarians; Daniel Isaac Eaton was a Paineite deist and republican; Irish Catholics and Dissenters rose together in 1798; John Thelwall was certainly not – as Roe proposes – a 'disciple' of Godwin, even if he borrowed from *Political Justice* in several lectures. And there were Foxite Whigs, Baptist pacifists, and even (James Montgomery of Sheffield) at least one Moravian.

There is a sense in which the espousal of Godwinism represented an actual retreat from immediate political commitment. The very utopianism of *Political Justice* appealed in characteristic ways to the revolting intelligentsia. It enabled them to pose as far more enlightened and revolutionary (in theory) than the next man, to call in question – not the mere ephemera of daily life, the war, the high prices of food in 1795, the taxes, the corrupt representation – but (as philosophers above such tedious matters) to question the State, Law, Punishment, Marriage, Property, the Lot. And it enabled them to distance their theoretic revolutionism from humdrum actuality. Godwin did not involve them in any allegiance towards any part of the messy French revolutionary process. He disclaimed all sympathy for agitational methods or the popular societies. When the Two Acts were passing through Parliament, Godwin came forward in a pamphlet over the name of 'A Lover of Order' to censure, not the ministers, but his friend John Thelwall, the Jacobin lecturer. 'Whether or no Political Lectures, upon fundamental principles of politics, to be delivered to a mixed and crowded audience be entitled to the approbation of an enlightened Statesman, it is somewhat difficult to pronounce.' But despite the difficulties, he was able to pronounce – against.

The pronouncement afforded legitimation, and from the ultra-radical wing, to the authors of the Two Acts. Godwin's proposed reforms – which included the abolition of the State and of private property – were, Thelwall commented, 'to be produced by writing quarto volumes, and conversing with a few speculative philosophers by the fireside'.

I should declare an interest here and make it clear that Roe and I disagree on the question of Godwin. He makes valid points against me as to Godwin's support for the accused in the treason trials, at a critical moment, and as to the philosopher's own undoubted exposure to the onslaughts of anti-Jacobinism. As I have said, the popular and the polite reform movements were brushing against each other all the time. Even the breach over the Two Acts was repaired the following autumn. A friend of Crabb Robinson's wrote to him from Norwich that Godwin and Thelwall had been in the city and had been reconciled: 'I have since seen them walking together round our Castle Hill. Of course the former will no longer be accused of 'cherishing a feebleness of spirit', nor will the latter be again compared to Iago. Like Gog and Magog they will now go hand in hand in their glorious schemes.'

Yet I have looked enough into private papers of young Godwinians of the time to know how shallow and posturing some of their revolutionism was. Perhaps this is true of the revolting intelligentsia in most ages and most places, not excluding our own. Many young intellectuals of this time sowed wild Godwinian oats for two or three years, suffered nothing for it in person or in self-esteem, did nothing to aid the actual movements for reform, served with alacrity in the Volunteers against plebeian food rioters, and ended as pillars of complacent Utilitarianism.

Godwinism had rather little to do with 'politics', and that is where the literary-critical stereotypes, both 'left' and 'right', go wrong. It was rather – just as Wordsworth was to describe it – a withdrawal from politics at the point at which aspiration had met with defeat, a retreat from the complexity and confusion of reality, a glissade from engagement to speculation: 'To abstract the hopes of man/Out of his feelings'. But, for a few, it was accompanied by authentic explorations of the intellectual dimensions of radicalism and by innovations in personal behaviour and relations. This had cultural consequences more profound than it had political.

Wordworth's crisis must surely be found somewhere in this contradictory milieu? There could well have been personal dimensions to this conflict, but these need not have taken any political form. Several of Wordsworth's advanced friends underwent profound crises at this time. Roe directs us to John Tweddell. He might have looked more closely than he does at Basil Montagu, with whom Wordsworth shared lodgings in 1795 in Lincoln's Inn. Montagu later wrote (somewhat cryptically) that Wordsworth saw him then 'perplexed and misled by passions wild and strong'. A mutual friend, Francis Wrangham, wrote, defensively, of him in a letter of 1799: 'Perhaps you will consider it as a fresh proof of his fickleness that he has at last determined to be steady – not *carried about* ...with every wind of doctrine – But, amidst all his fluctuations upon the wide ocean of opinion, he has never lost hold of his integrity – His humanity retained its warmth even in the frozen sea of Godwinism...' We see him momentarily in that frozen sea, like a whale coming up at a blowhole, in Joseph Farrington's diary, where Montagu 'seems to have imbibed in a violent degree the speculative principles of the new Philosophers. He pleaded against the existence of instinct, and said that Poets are made by education. That a Parent should not love his Child better than the Child of another, but in proportion as the Child might possess better qualities and endowments.'

It may be that at closer quarters Montagu was less

amiable. 'Two persons,' Hazlitt commented, in his portrait of
Godwin, 'agree to live together in Chambers on principles of
pure equality and mutual assistance – but when it comes to the
push, one of them finds that the other always insists on his
fetching water from the pump in Hare-court, and cleaning his
shoes for him.' That could perhaps be drawn from Montagu
and one of his pupils, perhaps John Pinney. Montagu's child,
little Basil, was shed onto William and Dorothy Wordsworth
at Racedown and the promised remittances for his care and
keep came to hand as rarely as did promised visits from his
father. Meanwhile Montagu was sponging on his friends
(including Wordsworth), on the Wedgwoods, and on his
pupils, and was courting Sarah Wedgwood and the £25,000
which went with her. Hazlitt once again (and this time he
could have had Wordsworth's loan to Montagu in mind): 'A
member of the *ideal* and perfect commonwealth of letters
lends another a hundred pounds for immediate and pressing
use; and when he applies for it again, the borrower has still
more need of it than he, and retains it for his own especial,
which is tantamount to the public, good. The Exchequer of
pure reason, like that of the State, never refunds.' In all these
affairs Montagu evidently felt the self-approbation of a true
Modern Philosopher. As he was eminently worthy of support
as a most talented member of society, so he was glad to
contribute to the happiness of his creditors by enabling them to
gratify their own benevolence by lending him money.
Wordsworth wrote grumpily some years later that Montagu
was a man whose conduct is 'little governed by the universally
admitted laws of Friendship and regulations of society'.
'Tempting region that,' the *Prelude* added,

> For Zeal to enter and refresh herself,
> Where passions had the privilege to work,
> And never hear the sound of their own names.

I am not trying to cast Montagu for a part in *The Borderers*. (David Erdman has recently found one good performer for that, in Colonel John Oswald.) But the 'false philosophy' undoubtedly had human attachments, and James Chandler is not going to persuade me that Wordsworth thought it all up while reading Rousseau. As for 'the whole tribe of authors' such as Godwin and Paley (Wordsworth decided at Goslar), 'these bald and naked reasonings are impotent over our habits, they cannot form them ...They contain no picture of human life, they describe nothing.' It is significant that Wordsworth rejects equally the revolutionary and the conservative philosopher. This is no movement from 'Left' to 'Right': if anything, it is a movement away from both, to an anti-politics or an anti-philosophy, or – as Chandler has it more happily in the title to one of his chapters – an 'Ideology against "Ideology" '.

The question, wrote Hazlitt, is 'whether benevolence, constructed upon a logical scale, would not be merely *nominal*, whether duty, raised to too lofty a pitch of refinement, might not sink into callous indifference or hollow selfishness?' And the questions stem not only from speculation but also from practical encounters with speculators; from the grotesque discrepancies between benevolent professions and petty self-interest; from the plain inadequacy of Reason to so many human situations. (As Mary Wollstonecraft lay dying, she regarded an interfering housemaid and pleaded with Godwin: 'Pray, pray, do not let her reason with me.') In this critical year Wordsworth had suffered some insight into moral nihilism – perhaps as much in his own nature as in that of his associates? – and he had found self-interest in the mask of reason, and self-love masked as philanthropy. There was a sudden motion of recoil, which took him from London to Racedown, Stowey and Goslar, and (in literary terms) from the 'Descriptive Sketches' to 'Salisbury Plain' and *The Borderers*.

The 'false philosophy' associated with the Godwinian milieu was seen as a threat to his vocation. It was not only Montagu in that circle who was arguing that 'poets are made by education.' The pre-programmed forced growth of 'genius' came up frequently for discussion. Godwin addressed the question in the *Enquirer*. There was to come, late in 1797, Tom Wedgwood's proposal for a 'Nursery of Genius', with Wordsworth and Coleridge proposed as possible tutors.

Although this proposal was discovered by David Erdman in 1956, it is passed over without mention by Roe. Yet one answer to plans for the mechanical manufacture of consciousness was to write a counter-statement as to how a child's and a youth's consciousness in fact were formed. For evidence, Wordsworth must look into himself. This was to lead to the *Prelude: or Growth of a Poet's Mind.* And in some sense 'a poet' stood for any person – for the unplanned and self-creative path of human personality, the emphasis not upon planned rationality but upon awe, fancy, mystery, play, idleness and 'nature'.

This has less to do with 'politics' than is generally supposed. It certainly entails a rejection of Godwinian speculative abstractions. But the error, so common in critical stereotypes, is to suppose that Godwinism was the only significant intellectual position on the 'left', just as some people suppose that Marxism is such today. It would follow from this error that if Wordsworth rejected Godwin he must have been moving to the 'right', whereas he could perfectly well have been moving back to a more engaged sympathy with the poor and with the victims of war. That is, indeed, my reading of Wordsworth's trajectory. As Wordsworth gained in poetic power, he can be seen to be centrally concerned with the creative identity of everyman. And that is his own reading of his trajectory, as offered in Book 12 of the 1805 *Prelude.* This book includes some of the most unqualified affirmations in the poem, affirmations which some world-weary critics must find too boring to read since they do not appear in their critical discourse. It was on the roads, talking to travellers, vagrants, the returned soldier, the poor, that Wordsworth found

> Hope to my hope, and to my pleasure peace,
> And steadiness; and healing and repose
> To every angry passion. There I heard,
> From mouths of lowly men and of obscure
> A tale of honour ...

In my view, Wordsworth remained an 'odious democrat' until after the Peace of Amiens, and his poems of national independence and liberty are often criticisms of the course of the French Revolution from the 'left', for its own self-betrayal. It is the equation Godwinism = True Radicalism which is wrong, and which Roe still has not got right. Very certainly Wordsworth later turned his hand to manipulating and falsifying his experience. One example is the cartoon character, the Solitary, in the *Excursion*. In an unfortunate moment Nicholas Roe makes the unlikely suggestion that Coleridge was the model for the Solitary. A much stronger case can be made for John Thelwall, to whose memory Roe dedicates his book, but to argue this would carry us into another essay. In any case, there is an important sense in which the Solitary was Wordsworth himself, or Wordsworth's Jacobinical alter ego, now extruded and disowned, placed out there as a caricature, defeated in every aspiration – indeed an examplar that all affirmative social aspirations must be delusions. As Hazlitt saw when he reviewed the *Excursion*, 'Wordsworth's thoughts are the real subject ...Even the dialogues ...are soliloquies of the same character, taking different views of the subject. The recluse, the pastor and the pedlar are three persons in one poet.' But even the dialogues are rigged. The Solitary has been beaten by every accident of life, beset by domestic tragedy, political defeat, philosophical bankruptcy. He is not allowed to answer back, as pedlar, parson and poet all set about him. And it should be remembered that the *Excursion* was published in 1814, whereas the *Prelude* lay in manuscript until Wordsworth's death in 1850. Yet it is only when we have the second in our hand that we have a key to the first.

I wish that I could have given Nicholas Roe's book a more enthusiastic review, since much work as gone into it, and it will become necessary reading among students of Wordsworth – its contribution to Coleridge studies is more slight. But by avoiding arguments with other critics his own views are left unclarified; his book becomes encumbered with detail and fails to suggest clearly the trajectory followed by each poet in the 1790s. If I wanted to show Wordsworth's trajectory to a keen novice today I would still send her back to read George McLean Harper.

BENEVOLENT MR GODWIN

A feast for the Godwinians. First comes the handsome facsimile of the quarto first edition of *Political Justice* (1793) in the series edited by Jonathan Wordsworth for Woodstock Books. This series makes available facsimiles of works which were significant to the Romantic poets, and in particular to Wordsworth and Coleridge. Jonathan Wordsworth's breezy and unpedantic introduction seeks to bring the reader into that circle at that time, so that s/he can place the two heavy volumes on a desk and be drawn into the self-satisfied philosophical benevolence and contempt for all received opinion and custom which inspired those young enthusiasts. We open them beside the solicitor's clerk, Henry Crabb Robinson, who later recalled: 'It made me feel more generously. I had never before, nor ...have I ever since felt so strongly the duty of not living to one's self, but of having for one's sole duty the good of the community.' The 1793 edition sold 3000 copies at the high price of three guineas – too pricey for the Government to worry about a prosecution. Woodstock Books will count itself fortunate if it can sell as many. At £150 it will also not be prosecuted.

Mark Philp has given himself a more difficult task. He has edited the new seven-volume edition of the *Political and Philosophical Writings of William Godwin*, having edited previously, with some help from Marilyn Butler, all of

Godwin's novels. Philp is undoubtedly the country's leading Godwinian, having established his authority with his study of *Political Justice*. He has perhaps become over-committed to the role, although he has also edited an interesting collection of essays on the French Revolution and British popular politics. The present series is a selection and not the complete output, and we may be thankful for that. It could have been pruned down more. I find Volume I – *Political Writings I* – superfluous, apart from the editor's general introduction to the series; as are Volumes VI, *Essays*, and VII, *Religious Writings*. These will be useful to the close scholar of Godwin's evolution, who might, however, have found the texts by other means. Most are dull texts.

My main complaint is that Dr Philp might have given more thought to the problems of editing and to the needs of his intended readership. The editing is not pedantic: indeed, compared with some series, such as the Bollingen Coleridge, it is lightweight. Each text has a two or three-page introduction: when it was published, where, what was the immediate response in reviews. Anything with a capital letter gets a footnote in explanation: thus we are told who Guy Fawkes was (twice), who was Caligula, Nebuchadnezzar, who were Goths and Vandals, what was the Inquisition, Pandora (box of) and Procrustes (bed of). We may live in a multicultural society but this is taking things a bit far. Readers who open these volumes will come with some preparation. But in any case Godwin is using all these terms as commonplace figures of speech and not as part of a historical enquiry. The volume from which most of these examples come – Volume II, *Political Writings II* – suffers from editorial brevity in other respects. It includes three significant interventions: the 'Cursory strictures on the charge delivered by Lord Chief Justice Eyre to the Grand Jury', Godwin's strong public protest – perhaps his most courageous literary act – against the nonsensical construction of the law of treason by Eyre (which has recently attracted renewed ironical attention from John Barrell) which was hurled into print on the very eve of the notorious Treason Trials of 1794. The second piece is the 'Considerations' on the Two Acts (1795), in which Godwin seemed to come forward (anonymously) to condone legislation against popular organisations like the Corresponding Societies and assemblies judged to be tumultuous (such as John Thelwall's public political lectures), while moaning on and on about Bills so loosely drawn that they might even touch benign philosophers like himself. The third piece, 'Thoughts occasioned by the perusal of Dr Parr's Spital Sermon' (1801), is more honourable. The intellectual tide had turned strongly against Godwin since 1797 and he had remained silent. Now at last he responded to some major critics, including Dr Parr, Mackintosh and Malthus.

On all three texts the editor is correct but less helpful than he could be. We get little sense of the point of crisis at which the first was thrown into the press, nor of its possible influence. For the second we are allowed a note of one page. This implies that the essay was generally well received – based on a rapid round-up of reviews – with only John Thelwall dissenting. (We are given a reference to Thelwall's *Tribune* but not to his private exchange of letters with Godwin, first published in 1906, in Cestre's *John Thelwall*.) My impression is very different. The campaign against the Two Acts was most extensive, as is evidenced by the volume of petitions and meetings against them, and it extended from Charles James Fox and the Whigs, and the intellectual Jacobins, to the popular societies. When Thelwall complained that Godwin, in renouncing all active agitation, proposed that the public mind was to be transformed 'by writing quarto volumes, and conversing with a few speculative philosophers by the fire side', he carried most reformers with him. It was Thelwall, not Godwin, who was the reformers' hero of the day. It was Thelwall who defied the Two Acts and who continued to give public lectures disguised as Classical history. Godwin was held to have let down the cause.

Of course, this cannot all go into an editorial note. But it is an episode which illustrated a parting of the ways between activist and philosophical reformers and which has recently received renewed attention from historians of political thought. The reader could have been more fully informed. As to the third text, the editor simply goes limp. He tells us almost nothing of Dr Samuel Parr, nor of his offending sermon, nor of his previous associations with Godwin, and almost nothing of Sir James Mackintosh's influential refutal of the 'new philosophy'. At £395 the reader expects a little more.

But the real test for an editor is the handling of the three editions of *Political Justice*, 1793, 1796 and 1798, together with such manuscript drafts and later memos as are recovered here. As is to be expected, Philp passes this test with flying colours. The 1793 text appears in Volume III and the variant texts in Volume IV. If the results remain confusing, that is because of the impossibility of the project. Godwin did not just rewrite whole chapters, he dropped some altogether, and moved others – or parts of others – to new places. De Quincey said that the second edition 'as regards principles is not a recast, but absolutely a travesty of the first'. He overstated the case. But no conveniently readable variorum edition can be put together from manuscripts so messed about. We must prop ourselves up with both volumes, and perhaps also with the final volume (which includes the consolidated index), and be thankful that Godwin found an editor with the patience to tease it all out.

Philp admires Godwin. He could scarcely have completed his task if he didn't. And he commends him for 'retaining a core of consistency of doctrine throughout his career'. What is this?

At the centre of Godwin's position is a commitment to a duty-based conception of morality, revolving around benevolence and a conception of utility couched in perfectionist terms, constrained by the right of private judgment and 'further fuelled by a commitment to the potential moral equality of mankind. It is this constellation of concepts and commitments which forms the heart of Godwin's doctrine, and which remains central to his work throughout his life.

This is also where his 'enduring relevance to political and moral philosophy lies'.

That is a considerable mouthful, and one may munch on these concepts, revolving couches, fuelled commitments and constellations for many an hour, while still finding them indigestible. Philp wishes us to see Godwin as making minor adjustments within a stable constellation, but something more drastic was involved in the revisions. From 1793 he was in retreat: as he revised the claim for perfectibility to the 'progressive nature of man'; as he came to lay stress on 'politeness' and showed more and more distaste for any revolutionary, tumultuous or plebeian reformers; as he found, belatedly, space for imagination and even for the domestic affections; as he gave in, with Wollstonecraft, to the Gothic institution of marriage, it was difficult for contemporaries to feel that he was aloft in the same constellation.

One star in that constellation might merit closer attention: 'benevolence'. Hazlitt also saw its central place: Godwin, he wrote, 'absolves man from the gross and narrow ties of sense, custom, authority, private and local attachments, in order that he may devote himself to the boundless pursuit of universal benevolence'. And this was certainly the way in which Godwin was taken by his young disciples. Still, in 1797, Crabb Robinson was writing to his brother: '*Our* Philosophy has freed us from a weighty pack of instincts & natural affections which antient philosophers have stuck upon the human frame

& constitution like burrs and patches.'

'Benevolence' can be chased back down 18th-century corridors to Shaftesbury and beyond, and up and down Hartleyan staircases, but one wonders how far it was a philosophical term of art at all and how far a social posture. If I may leave the philosophical high ground, this was borne in on me when I consulted a schoolgirl's diary, by one of the Quaker Gurneys of Norwich, who were very much caught up in the advanced thought of the time. Laura Gurney's diary, which she sometimes read aloud with friends, is an index to the approved yes-words and boo-words of the time (1797). Her brother, John, who had purloined her inkstand, got a decidedly poor reference: 'How I do hate real Tyrannicalness! ...How *dis*-improved he is!' On the other hand, she was very much taken by a young man named Pitchford (with whom she exchanged diary readings): 'I admire & love him ...because he is so *virtuous*, so *interesting, so democratical*, & so truly benevolent.' In the next week's entry this is a little qualified:

> I think Pitchford's finest characteristic is a universal sort of benevolence. I do not think it is quite universal though, for I think he is governed by his *private likes & dislikes*. He has too much party spirit to be perfectly benevolent. He says in his journal that his *benevolence* never ripens into *beneficence*.

What the young Godwinians were trying to establish for themselves was a supremely privileged position of wholly disinterested rationality; from which great height they could look down on their fellow beings, whether aristocratic or vulgar. It was from such a height that Mr Collins looked down on Caleb Williams at the end of that novel:

> I regard you as vicious; but I do not consider the vicious as proper objects of indignation and scorn. I consider you as a machine; you are not constituted, I am afraid, to be greatly useful to your fellow men: but you did not make yourself; you

101

are just what circumstance irresistibly compelled you to be. I am sorry for your ill properties; but I entertain no enmity to you, nothing but benevolence.

What a put-down! And, in the context of the novel, perhaps an irony against Godwin's own theories. But a correct record of them nonetheless. As Wordsworth was to recall, with greater irony, but not without reminiscent sympathy:

> What delight! -
> How glorious! – in self-knowledge and self-rule
> To look through all the frailties of the world,
> And with a resolute mastery shaking off
> The accidents of nature, time and place,
> That make up the weak being of the past,
> Build social freedom on its only base:
> The freedom of the individual mind,
> Which, to the blind restraint of general laws
> Superior, magisterially adopts
> One guide – the light of circumstances, flashed
> Upon an independent intellect.

How 'independent' could intellect be, however? In the Hartleyan tradition reason could coexist with paternalism: philanthropy or benevolence were synonymous with the gentry. But with Godwin benevolence has migrated to the radical intelligentsia. He does not write of it as the property of an educated middle class only: he writes of it rather as Reason, and it is a cardinal point that all men are capable of being liberated by Reason. But (he wrote in the *Enquirer*) the existing state of society is 'a state of slavery and imbecility'. 'It puts an end to that independence and individuality, which are the genuine characteristics of an intellectual existence, and without which nothing eminently honourable, generous or delightful can in any degree subsist.' Where is the social location of Reason in Godwin's time? Very clearly it must be among the enlightened intelligentsia. Only they can rise above 'circumstances' and attain to true independence.

If such terms are ever helpful there is no position which better deserves to be called 'bourgeois radical' than Godwin's. This can even be expressed, almost comically, in the form of equations. On the one hand, we have Gothic superstition/ habit/institutions (all these = aristocracy) sitting on top of Reason = Intelligentsia. On the other hand, we have Reason = Intelligentsia sitting on top of circumstances/ custom/ignorance = the plebs. Thus Reason was sandwiched between aristocratic institutions (above) and mob ignorance (below). When regarding the impediments of the first situation Godwin could view 'the people' with equanimity as allies: 'The real enemies of liberty in any country are not the people, but those higher orders who find their imaginary profit in a contrary system. Infuse just views into a certain number of the liberally educated and reflecting members; give to the people guides and instructors; and the business is done.' But Godwin has scarcely reached this optimistic point before he is racked by doubts: he remembers the second equation. And he immediately continues: 'This however is not to be accomplished but in a gradual manner.' And at once he turns to face the danger of popular societies, and the distastefulness of revolutions: 'During a period of revolution, enquiry, and all those patient speculations to which mankind are indebted for their greatest improvements, are suspended ...Such speculations demand leisure, and a tranquil and dispassionate temper; they can scarcely be pursued when all the passions of man are afloat.'

This, then, was the voice of an enlightened intelligentsia, with its virtues but also its arrogant vices. (To be fair, they had good reason to be cautious of the crowd, as they looked back on the Priestley Riots in Birmingham and countless burnings of Tom Paine in effigy.) Where does this leave 'benevolence'?

103

It could always be recommended for both public and private reasons. As a private virtue it brought its own reward in 'self-approbation': 'No man ever performed an act of exalted benevolence, without having sufficient reason to know, at least so long as the sensation was present to his mind, that all the gratifications of appetite were contemptible in comparison.' The public virtue of benevolence was its social utility – disinterested rational judgment and action for the benefit of society. But at the zenith of its popularity 'benevolence' began to lose its identity and to migrate from its first meaning to its second. As Godwin wrote in *Political Justice* (third edition): 'Morality is a system of conduct which is determined by a consideration of the greatest general good: he is entitled to the highest moral approbation, whose conduct is in the greatest number of instances ...governed by views of benevolence, and made subservient to public utility.' We are presented here with benevolence in a very different aspect: we have moved from self-approbation to public approbation, and from the rational intention of the individual to the exterior notion of a rational standard of utility out there, in society, to which the individual adjusts.

For a moment Godwin held this difficulty in his hand and frowned at it:

> Intention no doubt is of the essence of virtue. But it will not do alone. In deciding the merits of others, we are bound ...to proceed in the same manner as deciding the merits of inanimate substances. The turning point is their utility. Intention is of no further value than as it leads to utility: it is the means, and not the end.

Godwin has crossed a threshold here into utilitarianism, and utilitarianism of a bleak kind, with all its repetitious, self-satisfied abbreviations of history and culture. It was only necessary to wed his thought to the calculations of orthodox political economy (much as Bentham did) to have this new progeny. Godwin himself did not follow this to its final conclusion: he held fast, as a querulous utopian, but Philp's consistent 'constellation' looks very different. It was in alarm at this slippage that Wordsworth withdrew aghast. It seemed to him to be a matter less of rational argument than of sensibility. He could not read the second edition of *Political Justice* because of its 'execrable' style. In a very interesting note he turned away from the leading conservative and the leading radical philosopher on the same grounds:

> I consider such books as Mr Godwyn's, Mr Paley's and those of the whole tribe of authors of that class as impotent to all their intended good purposes ...I know no ...system of moral philosophy written with sufficient power to melt into our affections, to incorporate itself with the blood and vital juices of our minds ...These bald and naked reasonings are impotent over our habits, they cannot form them.

We must thank Jonathan Wordsworth and Mark Philp for enabling us to celebrate the bi-centenary of *Political Justice*. It was one of those rare moments when a section of the English intelligentsia called all things in question, and the vibrations were felt for decades. A most un-English moment. But what am I to do now with yet one more Pickering volume, Mary Wollstonecraft's *Political Writings*, comprising the *Vindication of the Rights of Woman,* her *Rights of Men*, and chapters from her unfinished history of the French Revolution? This is edited by Janet Todd, who previously edited, with Marilyn Butler, a seven-volume edition of Wollstonecraft. We did not need a new edition of the *Vindication*: there is a good one, thoughtfully edited by Miriam Brody, still on Penguin's lists. But it is useful to have available Wollstonecraft's sharp early polemical reply to Burke. It is not benevolent at all. Indeed, I do not like to put Godwin and Wollstonecraft together in the bed of the same review. I have never been able to understand how she got into that Sartre-De Beauvoir double act with him. Her sensibility was more ardent and volatile – she shared Wordsworth's distrust of 'bald and naked reasonings' – and she did not posture in Godwin's way. Intellectually she remained her own person, living in her separate establishment.

There comes down with this torrent of books yet one more – a neat and cheap paperback facsimile of Godwin's *Memoirs of Wollstonecraft*. This was flung into the press immediately following her death, when Godwin, for once, was deeply moved out of his habitual self-preoccupation. I have never been able to make my mind up whether this was an act of piety which met the claims they both made for open sincerity, or a blunder which exposed her to her enemies.

SAMUEL TAYLOR COLERIDGE

THE POET AND HIS EDITORS

BLISS WAS IT IN THAT DAWN –
THE MATTER OF COLERIDGE'S
REVOLUTIONARY YOUTH

Samuel Taylor Coleridge was in or around Bristol much of
1795 and 1796, in his twenty-third and twenty-fourth years.
He married, became a father, delivered two series of lectures
(an enterprise which he shared with Southey, nearly two years
his junior), and between March and mid-May 1796 he edited
ten numbers of a political and literary journal, *The Watchman*.

Some six or seven years after this he had substantially
shifted his positions, rejecting his Hartleian necessitarianism,
and repudiating his passionate (if ambiguous) alliance with the
democrats. Some parts of *The Friend*, in 1809, appear as an
argument with his own tousle-headed, impassioned, Bristol
youth. The argument was continued in *Biographia Literaria*
(1817) with such tergiversation that he succeeded in
convincing himself: the friends of his *Watchman* days (he
alleged) 'will bear witness for me how opposite even then my
principles were to those of Jacobinism or even of democracy'.
Although no such friends thrust themselves forward to give
this convenient testimony, the matter of Coleridge's youth was
already becoming enwrapped in a familiar Coleridgean
obscurity. Despite James Dykes Campbell's sober attempt to

assemble a factual account (first published in 1894 and now reprinted) and the numerous recoveries of recent scholars, some part of that obscurity has remained to the present day.

All but its last vestiges are now removed in two well-edited volumes of the *Collected Works* (under the general editorship of Kathleen Coburn), in which Peter Mann and Lewis Patton present the political and theological lectures of 1795 and *The Watchman*. Barbara Rooke's edition of *The Friend* has already appeared in this series and we await only David Erdman's edition of *Essays on His Times* (culled largely from the *Morning Post* and *Morning Chronicle*) to have a definitive view of Coleridge's evolution from 1795 into the early 1800s.*

William Blake apart, no English writer of the past 200 years can have been served by such an eminent congregation of North American and British scholarship. Apart from the *Collected Works* (and leaving aside many notable biographical and critical contributions), we now have the superlative edition of *The Notebooks* (by Kathleen Coburn), the more reticent edition of the *Collected Letters* (by Earl Leslie Griggs), and Carl Woodring's learned *Politics in the Poetry of Coleridge*. Coleridge, who completed so little work to his own final satisfaction in his own lifetime, and who, in any case, succeeded so rarely in giving to his ideas consistent and systematic organization, now appears laid open to view as a veritable literary Herculaneum, excavated by half a hundred highly skilled posthumous literary amanuenses. These two new volumes of the *Collected Works* both belong to the best tradition of this scholarship.

Coleridge is the very acme of the editor's author. As John

* See below p. 143 for review of the Erdman volume.

Livingston Lowes first showed in *The Road to Xanadu*, scarcely
a line came from Coleridge's pen which was not derivative of
some literary experience. Week after week, year in, year out,
this literary input continued; and week after week it returned,
well or ill assimilated, in letters, notebooks, poems, articles,
lectures. One of the fascinations of Coleridge is not in his
originality or force of intellect (which is too often overrated
by scholars who have a professional bias to confuse width of
reference with creative originality) but in the energetic catholicity
of his interests. Whatever happened, as a literary experience, in
the 1790s or early 1800s, turns up in some form in his writings:
every controversy, every philosophical hang-up, every new
literary mode, chance-hap millenarial prophets like Richard
Brothers, anti-Jacobin professionals like John Reeves, squalid
diplomatic deals with the King of Naples, voyages of discovery
– whatever was written about somehow caught his eye, was
ingested, and then thrown out again, usually in some oblique,
unpredictable context.

Everything is there. And hence the temptation to scholars
to use his texts, not in their own right, but as a clothes-line to
hang everything upon. And there are, indeed, long passages of
the 'Lectures on Revealed Religion' when Coleridge himself
is doing little else than stringing up other men's washing.
Bursting upon the Bristol scene as an impassioned reformer in
February, 1795 (his lecture 'On the Present War', published
in Conciones ad Populum, can – in the pamphlet literature of
1793 to the Peace of Amiens – be compared, in its tone of
absolute moral rage, only with a few passages of Gilbert
Wakefield, William Blake, or William Frend), he and
Southey gathered around themselves an audience which, in
all probability, was laced with young ultra-Godwinians,
necessitarians and deists. With a characteristic mixture of
courage, egoism, and perversity, Coleridge immediately set
out, in his theological lectures, to challenge the prejudices of

110

the 'infidels' among his supporters, by grounding his own idiosyncratic reformism upon Christian precept and revelation.

But – characteristically again – he could rarely get around to preparing each lecture until the day before. His borrowings from the Bristol Library are known, and, with the help of these records and of his own wide reading, Dr Mann's annotations show us Coleridge, like a young and harassed WEA lecturer, grabbing an armful of books at noon on the eve of a lecture, retiring to his lodgings, working through the night, and emerging with a (generally unfinished) manuscript at the eleventh hour before delivery. No wonder a friendly commentator noted that 'Mr C- would ...do well to appear with cleaner stockings in public, and if his hair were combed out ...it would not depreciate him in the esteem of his friends'. The wonder is that in this brief period of intense concentration he put together, not notes for a lecture, but a tolerable draft of its greater part.

This was done, however, at the cost of great intellectual indigestion. Whole paragraphs and even pages were copied, sometimes word for word, sometimes with significant revision, from the pile of half-gutted books at his elbow: from Hartley and Priestley, from Maclaurin on Newton, from Lowman on the *Civil Government of the Hebrews*, from Cudworth's *True Intellectual System of the Universe*, Balguy's *Divine Benevolence Asserted*, Michaelis's *Introduction to the New Testament*. In several cases Dr Mann notes that evidently only the first volume of a multi-volume work has been consulted.

There were six theological lectures, and much of the first four are taken up with a hotch-potch of derivative philosophy and Christian apologetics. Their interest (apart from serving as a guide to Coleridge's reading) lies in the manner in which Coleridge organized and deployed fragments of other men's thoughts, and in occasional prefatory or transitional passages which are wholly his own. Also of interest is that way in which Coleridge prepared the ground for a confrontation with Godwinian philosophy. On all these points Dr Mann is a percipient guide.

Carefully prepared as it was, the confrontation between Coleridge and Godwinism never came about. Often announced (in his letters, in his notebooks, in *The Watchman*) as the philosophic tourney of the decade, Coleridge always retired after a preliminary flamboyant canter around the field. Dr Mann insists at several points that the theological lectures dispose finally of the notion that Coleridge, in 1795, was an ardent disciple of Godwin. And he indicates very clearly those passages where Coleridge was beating the bounds between them – in particular, those many, echoing passages where Coleridge insists that benevolence must be nurtured, in the first place, by the 'home-born' feelings.

But to move from this to the suggestion that the issue is raised, in these lectures or in *The Watchman*, to the level of mature philosophical argument, is to read back into 1795-96 fifteen years of subsequent evolution. It is also to carry the work of an editorial amanuensis too far. Coleridge was in fact inhibited from offering this confrontation for two reasons, one temporary, the other to prove permanent. The first is that both Godwin and the Coleridge of 1795-96 derived their view of man's nature from common Hartleian (and sometimes Priestleyan) roots. So long as Coleridge moved within the premises of Hartleian necessitarianism, he was a prisoner to premises from which Godwin derived conclusions which he repudiated.

The second, more permanent, inhibition was a habit of impatience when arguing with deism or atheism: at a certain point, Coleridge would simply throw up his arms and pass over to rhetoric, often of a vulgar and bigoted kind . Atheism, for Coleridge, *must* indicate a capitulation to mere sensuality:

the matter is not argued, it is asserted as a commonplace. An atheist was 'an intellectual Deformity'. The theological lectures begin with a dream-sequence in which Sensuality and the Monster Blasphemy are discovered together in a 'Vast and dusky Cave'. The sensuality of the atheist was so axiomatic that (in the third lecture) Coleridge denies to him the possibility of aesthetic experience:

> to a Sensualist and to the Atheist that alone can be beautiful which promises a gratification to the appetite – for of wisdom and benevolence the Atheist denies the very existence. The Wine is beautiful to him when it sparkles in the Cup – and the Woman when she moves lasciviously in the Dance but the Rose that bends on its stalk, the Clouds that imbibe the setting sun – these are not beautiful.

In *Religious Musings* Coleridge had thrown in the line: 'Ye petrify the inbrothell'd Atheist's heart', and Thelwall quite properly took him to task for 'one of those illiberal & unfounded calumnies with which *Christian* meekness never yet disdained to supply the want of argument'. But neither then nor later did Coleridge learn to supply this want, when he came to a similar point in his argument. By denying dignity and sensibility to his opponent, he denied dignity and rigour to his own argument, and descended time and again to mere exclamation and apologetics.

At times he descended to something worse. When he exclaimed, after a vivid caricature of some notions in *Political Justice*, 'Your principles are villainous ones! I would not entrust my wife or sister to you – Think you, I would entrust my country?', he was descending to the very level of anti-libertarian and anti-intellectual lampoon which was the stock-in-trade of John Reeves and of the *Anti-Jacobin*: a kind of smear with which Mary Wollstonecraft was only too familiar. It was a kind of vulgarity with which Godwin, for all his cold-bloodedness, was never contaminated.

Fifteen years later Coleridge made an apology of a sort to Godwin: 'When I had read [your works] religious bigotry, the but half-understanding your principles, and the not half-understanding my own, combined to render me a warm & boisterous Anti-Godwinist.' So far, in a private letter, to Godwin. But in other private and public places he referred with increasing smugness to the fact that he, Samuel Taylor Coleridge, had never, for one moment, fallen into the ways of the Infidels. In March, 1798, he was writing to his brother, the Rev George Coleridge: 'I wish to be a good man & a Christian – but I am no Whig, no Reformist, no Republican.' In 1809 in *The Friend*: 'I may safely defy my worst enemy to shew, in any of my few writings, the least bias to Irreligion, Immorality, or Jacobinism.' And in that fine piece of fiction, chapter ten of *Biographia Literaria* (1817), he purported to explain the failure of *The Watchman*: 'I made enemies of all my Jacobin and democratic patrons ...disgusted by their infidelity and their adoption of French morals with French psilosophy [sic].' This is smug and smear together: his 'democratic patrons' were all immoral and all infidels; STC alone survived in purity.

The last two lectures on revealed religion (V and VI) are of greater originality and greater interest. The ghosts of these two cannot be exorcised by disclaimers in *The Friend* and *Biographia*. Bias to irreligion they may not show; but bias against the Established Church is to be found in plenty, and the later Coleridge – soliciting the Bishop of Llandaff's subscription for *The Friend*, and (in *Biographia*) celebrating Britain's good fortune in its Church establishment – must have been glad that they never got farther than manuscript. As a radical Dissenter, young Coleridge wished to show the infidels among his auditors that they were taking up arms, not against the Christian revelation, but against its manifold corruptions in the worldly churches: 'They may not determine against Christianity from arguments applicable to its' Corruptions only.' The rhetoric of Lecture V is one with which William Blake also was familiar:

> He who sees any real difference between the Church of Rome and the Church of England possesses optics which I do not possess – the mark of antichrist is on both of them. Have not both an intimate alliance with the powers of this World, which Jesus positively forbids? Are they not both decked with gold and precious stones? Is there not written on both their Foreheads Mystery? Do they not both SELL the Gospel – Nay, nay, they neither sell, nor is it the Gospel – they forcibly exchange Blasphemy for the first fruits, and snatching the scanty Bread from the poor Man's Mouth they cram their lying Legends down his Throat!

This – with more imagery of the Whore and 'Mother of Abomination' – is written hastily; one supposes after an all-night session, hair tousled, linen unkempt; and a paragraph or two later the manuscript breaks off. But this is Coleridge *talking* sedition, in a way in which his colleagues of those years were to remember, but in a way in which it was neither prudent nor (in the prosecuting climate of 1795-96) possible to go into print. The customary teasing, paradoxes and involuted ambiguities of the printed page are not present. He speaks, *tout court*, of 'the idolatrous doctrine of the Trinity, and the more pernicious dogma of Redemption'.

This is the Coleridge who loathed black vestments, and who preferred to preach, in Dissenting meeting-houses, in a blue coat with brass buttons; who could refer in his (late 1795) lecture, 'The Plot Discovered', to 'whole flights of Priests and Bishops, black men, and black men with white arms, like magpies and crows that pick out the eyes of sheep'; and who was not above writing slyly to a fellow Dissenter, during his tour to solicit subscribers for *The Watchman*, that his occasional sermons were helping forward his editorial business: 'The Sacred may eventually help off the *profane* – and my *Sermons* spread a sort of sanctity over my *Sedition*.'

'I know he cannot preach very often', John Thelwall hazarded early in 1798, 'without travelling from the pulpit to the Tower.' And the final lecture (VI) explains this judgment too. For Coleridge, still under his pantisocratic impulse sketched out – with references to Moses Lowman's version of Hebraic agrarian law (previously set out in Lecture II) – a critique of the institutions of property (and, in particular, of commercial imperialism and industrialization) in the light of a visionary communistic republic. His critique of society is based, not upon abstract Painite demands for equality of political right, but upon a wider claim for socio-economic equality.

This had already been set forward in *Conciones ad Populum*; arguing with the comfortable middle-class radical, with his faith in political machinery, Coleridge had declared:

> It is a mockery of our fellow creatures' wrongs to call them equal in rights, when by the bitter compulsion of their wants we make them inferior to us in all that can soften the heart, or dignify the understanding.

The same point is central to Lecture VI:

> The poor Infant born in an English or Irish Hovel breathes indeed the air and partakes the Light of Heaven: but of its other bounties he is disinherited. The powers of intellect are given him in vain – To make him work like a brute beast he is kept as ignorant as a brute beast.

Every level of society is polluted: 'Selfishness is planted in every bosom, and prepares us for the Slavery which it introduces.' At the point where the lecture appears to be moving towards a communistic peroration, it breaks off.

Whatever is made of this fragment, it certainly qualifies in a devastating way the extraordinary, and pat, opening to Essay VI of *The Friend*: 'From my earliest manhood it was an axiom in Politics with me, that in every country where property prevailed, property must be the grand basis of the government.' But we must leave further reflection upon these interesting recoveries to the reader's judgment, prompted by Dr Mann's excellent editorial advice.

The rest of these two volumes of the *Collected Works* – *The Watchman, Conciones, The Plot Discovered*, &c – are Coleridge's more direct political journalism of these two years. The writings have always been available, if inaccessible; and are adequately presented by Professor Patton, with some useful appendixes of contemporary documents.

He is especially helpful in presenting *The Watchman* in perspective. The legend has grown that, owing to Coleridge's unworldliness and his erratic alternations of indolence and energy, The Watchman was a shoddy production, always late for the printer, increasingly chucked together from cannibalizations from the general press. Professor Patton shows, on the contrary, that (despite some innocence in business experience) Coleridge ran, for ten numbers, a competent and regular politico literary miscellany. His borrowings from other journals were no more than eighteenth-century convention allowed. Moreover, the extracts from parliamentary debates and national newspapers, far from being chucked in haphazard to make up copy, were an important part of the initial intention of the periodical (to keep provincial reformers alert to important political developments in England and France) and – in their selection, abridgement, and editing – cost Coleridge as much effort as did the original contributions.

To reinforce this judgment, certain other comments may be added. The idea for *The Watchman* took fire at a unique moment in the 1790s, during the temporary solidarity brought about among all brands of disputing reformers (Foxites and plebeian democrats, Dissenters and 'infidels') by the campaign against the Two Acts. The Midlands and the West Country had been active in this great agitation, and the audience for a periodical seemed to lie ready to hand. The cause was self-evident, and dictated the title. 'Watchman' echoed through many passages of Isaiah and Ezekiel which were beloved by Dissent, and which set Coleridge happily in a prophetic role:

> I have set watchmen upon thy walls, O Jerusalem, which shall never hold their peace day nor night; ye that make mention of the Lord, keep not silence ...

Yet three months later, when *The Watchman* eventually appeared, the solidarities of December, 1795 had dispersed, and reformers and opponents of the French War were already withdrawing indoors. The chilly dusk of persecution was upon them, and the night of oppressive orthodoxy, which stretched from 1798 to the last years of the wars, lay ahead. Few radical journals survived 1796. Thelwall's *Tribune* concluded in April, 1796. In Sheffield, James Montgomery, the editor of the *Iris*, was in prison. In Norwich a miscellany appealing to a similar provincial audience, *The Cabinet*, had closed at the end of 1795. The attempt of leading members of the London Corresponding Society to run a *Moral and Political Magazine* in 1796 ended, despite the claims upon the loyalty of the society's membership, in disaster – a disaster which, in the view of Francis Place, struck a crippling blow at the society's finances. There need be no wonder that Coleridge got no farther than the tenth number. When additional difficulties are considered (the demands of his young household, the fact that his London bookseller refused to send any money for numbers sold), it is surprising that he got as far as he did.

The available audience was probably only large enough

to support the two journals towards which Coleridge guided his readers in his valedictory essay: the discreet *Monthly Magazine* (in which Dissenting reviewers took in Dissenting washing) and Benjamin Flower's pugnacious *Cambridge Intelligencer*, which had far better coverage of the news and commentary of interest to reformers than Coleridge could command. But, small as it was, this audience was of real importance. It is the failure of the editors to locate this audience which constitutes the only substantial criticism of their work. Indeed, so far from removing the last vestiges of obscurity about Coleridge's political position in 1795-96, they have actually added new misunderstandings of their own.

It will never to possible to write down the names and addresses of Coleridge's supporters in these years. No subscribers' lists have survived for *The Watchman*, as they have, by good fortune, for *The Friend*. However, even without such aids, Coleridge's intellectual reference-group need not be in doubt. Generations of literary critics have established the convention that Godwinism was coterminous with intellectual ultra-radicalism; and that any intellectual who signalled a major disagreement with Godwin must thereby have been moving away from the 'left'. Godwin occupies so important a place in mainstream intellectual history (the history represented by hardback publications and monthly or quarterly reviews) that this misunderstanding is easily made. But the attentive reader of the *Morning Chronicle*, the *Iris*, the *Cambridge Intelligencer*, the pamphlets and correspondence of the time will get a very different view. For many provincial reformers, Godwinism was neither here nor there: it was an exalted argument carried on in London. Alternative radical vocabularies lay to hand in the Lockean celebration of the Glorious Revolution; in plain Painism; or in the radical traditions of Christian Dissent. Godwin, by disclaiming political societies and activism, and by ducking the whole question of

France, had nothing to offer to middle-class sympathizers with the Norwich or Sheffield 'patriotic' societies. Indeed, the typical young Godwinian, like Wordsworth's friend Montagu, was too busy discussing universal benevolence to get into the rough-and-tumble of political argument: petitions against the Two Acts, public lectures, *The Watchman*, agitation against the war.

He was also too canny. Godwin was victimized by scandal and lampoon, but he was never brought to trial, to be transported or imprisoned, as were Thomas Fysshe Palmer, William Winterbottom, or Gilbert Wakefield. A number of these radical Christians had a quality of commitment which the authorities sense as more dangerous than the most advanced philosophical radicalism. In 1795 there was a small, but significant, new wave of this commitment among the young, who had their heroes (in Gerald, or Palmer, or William Frend), who lamented the hounding of Priestley out of the country, and who began to throw up spokesmen of their own.

Coleridge was exactly such a spokesman: his position was difficult, but it was by no means unique, nor was he as isolated as he later came to pretend. This can be seen in page after page of *University Rebel*, Frida Knight's very lively new life of William Frend. In matters of scholarship Mrs Knight belongs to a different league from Dr Mann and Professor Patton: her style occasionally is novelettish; she has received no grants from the Bollingen or other foundations. She is an 'amateur' historian (that is, unpaid), who has already written a sound study of Thomas Walker, the Manchester reformer.

Her book is a triumph. Year after year the North Atlantic ocean is darkened by the wings of migrating scholars – the English flying over to scrutinize (English) manuscripts secreted in the Huntington Library, the Berg Collection, the Pierpont Morgan or the Pforzheimer; the American scholars crowding out the British Museum or moaning at the lack of scholastic technology at Dove Cottage. Meanwhile Frida Knight has got on a bicycle (or perhaps a telephone) and tracked down two important collections of William Frend's letters, in the hospitable keeping of two descendants, as well as important related material in lesser collections including the Ely Diocesan Records. Her work is a very salutary reminder that, despite wars and salvage drives, much important material from the 1790s onwards survives in private attics; and that the real finds in scholarship lie off the main migration routes, and fall only to those with persistence and tact.

From these materials she has written a most readable book. It flags in the second half: partly because her subject flags, but partly because she is interested in the drama of William Frend, the intrepid radical drummed out of Cambridge after a ludicrous mock-trial in the Vice-Chancellor's court in 1793, and she fails to show the same interest in Frend's unitarian thought. She has the same quality as she gives to one of her own characters – 'a refreshing tendency to disregard points of doctrine in favour of general truths' – but since Frend himself was much concerned with doctrine, this is sometimes a disqualification. At such points she dives off into her store of letters, and produces a few pages of personalia: but personalia so vivid that we might be sitting at Frend's elbow.

Frend, as she shows, overplayed the drama of his 'trial', and failed to make of it the principled occasion which it might have been. He had neither the experience nor the temperament to carry such public notoriety. But he emerged quite uncompromised; exalted in the eyes of those students who, like Coleridge, had supported him; and as he matured (in banishment from the University) his naive integrity and his unheated intransigence carried him as far as the London Corresponding Society, for which he spoke and for whose prisoners he collected money.

Earlier, when Frend's scruples about the Trinity had led him to resign his curacy, he had exchanged the clerical black for a blue coat with brass buttons: such a coat as Coleridge preached sedition in during 1795. If we wish to plot Coleridge's position in the intellectual firmament in 1795 it is far more important to take bearings on Frend than on Godwin. It is also important to take more accurate bearings than Dr Mann and Professor Patton do upon the popular reform movement. On this point, the 'amateur' has a better sense of the times than the professional scholars.

Coleridge had been drawn into the great agitation against the Two Acts and he had no doubt jostled against the elbows of hundreds of new allies, reformers of all degrees. The Prospectus of *The Watchman* explicitly declares that

> it's chief objects are to co-operate (1) with the WHIG CLUB in procuring a repeal [of the Two Acts] and (2) with the PATRIOTIC SOCIETIES, for obtaining a Right of Suffrage general and frequent.

Professor Patton has something to tell us about the Whig Club, but, although he is normally so voluble, he refuses the second fence altogether. In the editors' joint introduction to the *Lectures* the failure to look steadily at the same point enlarges the area of misunderstanding. Coleridge's attitude to Godwinism, it is suggested, 'affected his attitude to the whole radical movement that had come into existence in the 1790s'; and:

> He was much distressed by the thought that Godwin's disciples, or radicals infected with Godwinian ideas, could be capturing the leadership of the people. Holcroft, for example ...played a leading role in the activities of the London Corresponding Society.

'It was the power of such men and their influence on the

masses that claimed Coleridge's fearful attention ...' Holcroft played no role in the LCS and probably was never a member. He had supported the more genteel Society for Constitutional Information which (like the Friends of the People) had ceased to have any national presence by 1795. Godwin had never supported the popular 'patriotic societies', by which all England understood, in 1795, those numerous provincial centres of democratic 'mischief' of which the LCS was the metropolitan mother. Indeed, he chose the moment of agitation against the Two Acts to single out the LCS and the popular tribune, John Thelwall, for specific attack. 'Ordinarily', propound the editors, Coleridge 'would have shared Godwin's fear of associations', but he was overborne by enthusiasm at the time of the Acts to join with their members in common agitation. They have no warrant for this proposition; nor can one easily see how they are able to decide what an eccentric and unstable twenty-three-year-old would 'ordinarily' do in time of national emergency.

What one *knows,* from the record, is less than this. We know that Coleridge, in 1795, chose – like John Thelwall in London – the open method of proselytizing public lectures: one clause in the Two Acts was specifically aimed at such lecturing, and Coleridge once suggested that government had been aiming not only at Thelwall but also at himself. We know that Coleridge was a star orator in the Bristol agitation against the Acts. We know that the prospectus to *The Watchman* specifically announced cooperation with the patriotic societies. And in *The Watchman* itself several telling contributions (sent in by the Rev John Edwards, another Frend-like Christian, and Priestley's successor at the Birmingham Meeting) gave a sympathetic blow-by-blow account of the persecution, under the Acts, of Binns and Gale Jones, the 'missionaries' of the LCS. And we know that in 1796 Coleridge began a warm correspondence with the people's tribune, John Thelwall.

Taken together, these facts suggest that the curve of Coleridge's commitment, in 1795-96, took him very close indeed to the popular societies – or towards their more intellectual component. If he was moving away from Godwin with his aloof élitism and his canny avoidance of persecution, he might, in these years, have been moving towards political activism, like his mentor, William Frend. Indeed, to publish *The Watchman*, and to travel the provinces for subscribers, is evidence of exactly such a stance.

By neglecting the alternatives to Godwinism, the editors discourage such a reading; and they leave us with a Coleridge who is a total individualist, in a unique posture, swatting hostile ideologies like wasps on every side. They support their reading with negatives: 'No evidence has been found that (patriotic) societies in 1795 were at all active in Bristol.' Perhaps not: historians have been less helpful on such points than they might have been. But there was a lusty Bristol Constitutional Society in 1794, small in numbers but confident: 'It is our firm opinion', they wrote to the LCS, 'could we but arouse them, that patriots would become nearly the majority of our city.' There is no reason to suppose that the society had ceased in 1795; it showed signs of activity as late as 1797. Certainly, the tone of Coleridge's letter to George Dyer in February, 1795, does not suggest that his lectures were delivered in an unformed political context:

I have endeavoured to disseminate Truth by three political Lectures ...But the opposition of the Aristocrats is so furious and determined, that I begin to fear, that the Good I do is not proportionate to the Evil I occasion – Mobs and Mayors, Blockheads and Brickbats, Placards and Press gangs have leagued in horrible Conspiracy against me – The Democrats are as sturdy in the support of me – but their number is comparatively small ...

'Uncouth and unbrained Automata' had scarcely been restrained 'from attacking the house in which the "damn'd Jacobine was jawing away" '.

It is more than probable that the Bristol of 1795-96 had, like Manchester, Nottingham, or Norwich, some more or less formal organization of reformers: perhaps overlapping circles – polite reading-groups and discussion clubs, some of whose more ardent members also supported a more popular reform society. Very possibly these 'democrats' would have supported Southey and Coleridge in their lectures, gathered signatures against the Acts, and bought *The Watchman*. But the editors are determined to leave Coleridge floating weightless in political outer space, subject to no atmosphere or force save the repulsion of Godwin and the remote gravitational pull of Burke.

In support of their reading they bring to bear several passages from Coleridge's own letters which should not have been employed without more careful critical scrutiny. Writing to Charles Lloyd's father, late in 1796, he referred to 'politicians and politics – a set of men and a kind of study which I deem highly unfavourable to all Christian graces'. But this sentence, alongside much other pious humbug, comes from a letter in which the author was attempting to calm the anxieties of a conventionally-minded father, whose disturbed son Coleridge had recently taken under his roof and patronage. It is no more useful as evidence than a phrase from one of those numerous calming letters which young lecturers in English or Sociology are no doubt at this moment indicting to parents in a similar predicament:

> While appreciating that it is sanctioned in youth culture, I myself have for long discouraged my students from the use of cannabis and other narcotics. Julia's idealism does her credit, but I am sure she will soon outgrow the practical revolutionism of misguided sects ...

If critics properly demand a discipline of reading (these words in this order), historians must with equal propriety demand their own discipline (these words in this context). And with no one is this discipline more necessary than with Coleridge, who combined a sensitive and often exciting ambivalence of attitude with a chameleon-like capacity to modify the colour of his opinions according to his correspondent. It is greatly disheartening to find Dr Mann concluding his acute and learned preface to the *Lectures* with the uncritical use of whole passages of the notorious letter which Coleridge wrote in October, 1803, when he had just heard of Emmett's death, to Sir George Beaumont. The event recalled to him, with acute shock, his own agitational youth:

> Fortunately for me, the Government, I suppose, knew that both Southey & I were utterly unconnected with any party or club or society ...I disclaimed all these Societies, these Imperia in Imperio, these Ascarides in the Bowels of the State ...All such Societies, under whatever name, I abhorred as wicked Conspiracies.

This, and so much more – an incoherent, contradictory, torrent of self-exculpation – is evidence only about Coleridge's state of mind in October, 1803. Not a sentence in that letter has any worth whatsoever as historical evidence, unless confirmed by other sources. As autobiography it is wholly corrupt. One is not, of course, labouring the petty point whether Coleridge was a card-holding member of a Bristol Constitutional Society or not. If there was such a society, it was probably so loosely organized that it did not have cards; and if it had, Coleridge probably forgot or on some scruple or other refused to join it. The point is the trajectory of Coleridge's allegiances in these years. And this (we have suggested) the editors have at this point obscured. It came very close to that of William Frend and of Gilbert Wakefield; and such a trajectory, if it had not been arrested by the retirement to Stowey, would almost certainly have led him to prison.

It was not only Hazlitt who remembered him as an ardent seditionist, until as late as 1797. When Coleridge denied his Jacobin sympathies in *The Friend*, Southey remarked: 'If he was not a Jacobine, in the common acceptation of the name, I wonder who the Devil was.' The editors dismiss this comment as 'spleen'; but there are others, which they overlook, which still have to be explained away. Professor Pollin has recently brought to light Thelwall's annotated copy of *Biographia*: where Coleridge wrote 'how opposite even then my principles were to those of jacobinism or even of democracy', Thelwall exclaimed: 'Mr C. was indeed far from Democracy, because he was far beyond it, I well remember – for he was a down right zealous leveller.' There is ample testimony of the way in which Coleridge's verbal sedition shocked the primmer relatives of Thomas Poole at Stowey. Fifty years later an old clergyman in the Quantocks was still found to be clucking over the 'sad democratic nonsense' talked by Coleridge in those days:

> 'It was a time of great political excitement, and, you see, we didn't change our opinions, but they did', said the vicar with a twinkle in his eye ...

One would not wish to deprive the vicar of his small octogenarian triumph: but perhaps he had misunderstood Coleridge's meaning? If so, then someone rather closer to Coleridge had fallen into the same misunderstanding. In April, 1799, the unhappy Sara (with Samuel in Germany) was under the necessity of applying to Poole for aid to pay the household bills:

> My principal reason for troubling you now is, to beg you will send me ten guineas, for I expected Coleridge would have thought of it, but he has not ...

The letter had two irritable postscripts. First: 'The Lyrical Ballads are not liked at all by any.' And the second: 'It is very unpleasant to me to be often asked if Coleridge has changed his political sentiments, for I know not properly how to reply. Pray furnish me.' No doubt the admirable Poole furnished the ten guineas, and 170 years of scholarship have done something to assuage the first postscript. But, in the matter of the second, Sara is still awaiting a definitive answer.

The editors do not finally 'furnish' Sara. Their command of intellectual history is impressive, and Dr Mann, in his editorial introduction, clarifies much. He insists properly upon the unitary development of Coleridge's thought, even where that unity is the exfoliation of successive interrelated ambiguities. From these first lectures onwards there can be traced consistencies of preoccupation. As Dr Mann writes:

> The fundamental emphases in his religious and political thinking that the lectures reveal suggest that his early work could be more accurately and justly seen as an intellectual reaction against the philosophy of the revolution, sharing the moral and social concern of the revolution, certainly, but resisting some of its most important controlling ideas about the individual, society, and religion as they appeared, at least, in the work of Godwin and Paine.

This is just; and, provided that one bears in mind that the 'philosophy of the revolution' is identified with Godwin/Paine, the point is proved. But if this proviso – a proviso which might be applied with equal validity to that other revolutionary, William Blake – is forgotten, one could be led on to false conclusions. Dr Mann writes that Coleridge's 'later intellectual progress can be seen not simply as an apostasizing rejection of his ideas of 1795, but as a more profound exploration and development of them'. Yes; but an exploration and development in only *one* of several possible directions; and in a direction which involved a distinct apostasy towards other alternatives and, indeed, towards some of that 'moral and social concern' which had illuminated his youth.

For in the glowing paradoxes of his notebooks, lectures and letters of these years, one has glimpses of abundant alternative possibilities of development: Coleridge the millenarian, Coleridge the communitarian Christian, Coleridge the revolutionary (rather than Burkean) critic of utilitarianism. Coleridge astonishes one, between 1794 and 1798, because of his capacity to contain within himself so many oscillating, contradictory philosophical impulses, each one momentarily realized, in a flash of illumination. If we speak of 'exploration and development' we must also speak of limitation and rejection. And the question of apostasy remains important, not because one wishes to nag at his biographers but because only this sense of covert self-betrayal explains the vehemence, the guilt-ridden and tortuous incoherence, of some of his later writings when he approached this sensitive area.

The contradiction in which Coleridge was immersed in 1795-96 was not only philosophical: it was also social. He was a utopian revolutionary who, nevertheless, was profoundly nervous of 'the mob' and who could see hope only in converting his own class or, at most, the educated and moralized artisan. However far these writings go in extremes of *opinion*, they show consistency at this point. In *The Watchman* (VI) he was writing of 'that greatest of evils, a revolution begotten by an unprincipled and extravagant government on a miserable, ignorant, and wicked people'. (Twenty years later he had forgotten about paternity, and wrote of revolutions as if they were malodorous virgin births.) In his antiwar lecture of 1795 (in *Conciones ad Populum*) his abuse of the putative father, William Pitt, went beyond all measure:

Heaven has bestowed on that man a portion of its ubiquity, and given him an actual presence in the Sacraments of Hell, wherever administered, in all the bread of bitterness, in all the cups of blood.

But in the same lecture he warned that the avowal of political truth should be made only among those 'whose minds are susceptible of reasoning: and never to the multitude, who ignorant and needy must necessarily act from the impulse of inflamed Passions'. 'General Illumination should precede Revolution', and the 'small but glorious band ...of thinking and disinterested Patriots' should 'plead *for* the Oppressed, not *to* them'.

The self-isolation of a utopian intellectual revolutionary has rarely been more explicitly defined. But the powerful pressures in experience which led Coleridge to this position are not always borne in mind. The crowd did not, in 1795, offer itself in England as any kind of organized democratic force. It was the mob of the Gordon Riots: the Church-and-King mob which, only four years before, had burnt down Priestley's laboratory: the price-fixing crowd which, historically, had often turned against Dissenting and Quaker corn merchants, and which throughout 1795 was clamouring against the middle-men: the Church-and-King bullies who attacked the meetings of patriotic societies (whose membership, if plebeian, was selected from a self-educated, self-respecting élite), and which was scarcely restrained from beating at Coleridge's own lecture-room doors. And if he turned to France, the mob also seemed to be an engine of destruction, pulling down impartially aristocratic privilege and the utopian hopes of the middle-class republican. As he wrote in *Conciones*,

The Annals of the French Revolution have recorded in Letters of Blood, that the Knowledge of the Few cannot counteract the

Ignorance of the Many; that the Light of Philosophy, when it is confined to a small Minority, points out the Possessors as the Victims, rather than the Illuminators, of the Multitude.

The communistic revolution of his 'theological' lectures must be preceded by a moral revolution within each individual:

> Let us exert over our own hearts a virtuous despotism, and lead our own Passions in triumph, and then we shall want neither Monarch nor General. If we would have no Nero without, we must place a Caesar within us, and that Caesar must be Religion.

From this position, a bridge might easily be thrown forward, across which he might pass, evacuating his youthful utopianism and occupying the territory of Burke and of the Established Church. But these recovered lectures establish firmly the seditious levelling of the lands he left behind. In Thelwall's copy of *Biographia* at the line, 'I retired to a cottage at Stowey', there is this marginal annotation:

> Where I visitted him & found him a decided Leveller – abusing the democrats for their hypocritical moderatism, in pretending to be willing to give the people equality of privileges & rank, while, at the same time, they would refuse them all that the others could be valuable for – equality of property – or rather abolition of all property.

Still, in 1797, Coleridge's criticism of the revolution was from the 'left'. But the watchman had left his post, and the night was coming on, not only without but also within. The watchman's uniform, the blue coat with brass buttons, was, no doubt, packed away in one of Sara's trunks. It was not to be the last time that the leftist intellectual critic was to find, in the impotence of his own self-isolation, an excuse for a reconciliation with the status quo. The undulating Quantocks were more inviting than Botany Bay; the great elms around the church tower at Stowey were an image of greater security than the banks of the Susquehanna. In July, 1797, he was visited by John Thelwall, and they settled down to talk in a quiet dell among the hills. 'Citizen John', said Coleridge, 'this is a fine place to talk treason in.' 'Nay! Citizen Samuel', Thelwall replied, 'it is rather a place to make a man forget that there is any necessity for treason.'

THE LIGHT AND THE DARK

By 1808 Coleridge had lost much of his early ebullience. The young man who jumped over a gate in his eagerness to be with the Wordsworths had changed into the staider figure whom De Quincey encountered under a gateway in Bridgwater, rousing himself with difficulty from his state of reverie. The eloquence, once set in motion, was as astonishing as before – 'like some great river, the Orellana, or the St Lawrence', said De Quincey – but a certain element of self-hypnosis was now involved as Coleridge sought to master or elude the contradictions which threatened to throttle his emotional and intellectual life. For the next dozen years he would be trying different expedients in an attempt to achieve the 'great work' that should justify his years of reading and inquiry.

It is these years that are covered by the new volume of his Notebooks – a volume which marks the greatest editorial triumph of the series so far, since the intermingling currents of Coleridge's thought reach a new intricacy, requiring voluminous annotation. Kathleen Coburn shows herself fully equal to their demands. As the work proceeds she has found it possible to allow herself more elbow-room in the notes. If Coleridge refers to an author, we can be sure that Professor Coburn will have looked out the work, traced the edition and summarized its relevance. If Coleridge says that a passage cannot be transcribed in full, the deficiency will invariably be found remedied in the annotation. At every point attention is drawn to parallel usages of particular terms, further discussions of issues, possible sources in Coleridge's reading. Yet the whole is done with tact and an unwillingness to interpret beyond the sufferance of the text. One of the happiest devices is the use of the speculative question, which avoids the clumsiness of such phrases as 'it may reasonably be suggested that ...' in all their variations.

The editor handles Coleridge's private life with discretion, offering the evidence yet refraining from sweeping judgment or hasty psychological analysis. Perceptively, she begins the new sequence with an entry in which, contemplating the ruinous effects of his relationship with the Wordsworth household, Coleridge comments: 'What remains? – to do them all the good, I can; but with a blank heart!' The 'still I gaze – and with how blank an eye!' of 'Dejection' has now generalized itself to cover a larger sphere of his actions: and this helps to explain the more complex mode of thought which is being deployed in these notes. Earlier his ranging sensibility was often content to exercise itself directly; now it tends to run underground, emerging less frequently in direct brilliance.

The general reader who dips here and there will find some ideas and observations which sparkle suggestively in their own right; in other cases he will need further guidance before the significance of a note becomes clear. The train of thought is so complex that sometimes annotation, however copious, is not enough. More often it is a matter of seeing the large pattern of significance that has prompted a particular entry. Coleridge reports an observation that fruit stains will easily wash out from a fabric so long as the fruit remains in season, but become indelible if delayed beyond that time. This item, no more than an interesting tit-bit in itself, assumes fuller significance when read in the context of earlier speculations concerning the possible sympathies between various manifestations of life. He speaks of his 'all-zermalming' (all-crushing), argument on the subject of ghosts, apparitions and so on; the jocular tone should not obscure the fact that the theory he then expounds concerning the powers of the 'imagination, the inward creatrix' to impose an interpretative pattern on sensations otherwise incomprehensible (a powerful factor, he argues, in the production of nightmares) contains some of his most fruitful ideas. Earlier hopes that study of such mental phenomena might help to illuminate the significance of religion itself persist, moreover; in 1810, he is still hoping to write a treatise entitled 'The Mysteries of Christianity grounded in, and correspondent to, the Mysteries of Human Nature'.

There are also some arid patches. The judicious reader learns to turn the page quickly when he sees a diagram or an attempt to verify the authenticity of Genesis. Yet not too quickly: 'anything', as Virginia Woolf remarked, 'may tumble out of that great maw'.

The new entries throw further light on that crisis of his personal life which culminated in the quarrel with Wordsworth. In its beginnings, his love for Wordsworth's sister-in-law, Sara Hutchinson, backed by his faith that a pure love, energetically cultivated, would necessarily be a source of inspiration, had seemed to promise new richness of creativity; over the years, with no prospect of a consummated relationship, it had become agonizing and artistically numbing. In its later stages, also, Coleridge recorded in his notebooks the occurrence of such unwelcome passions as an 'involuntary jealousy' towards Wordsworth (who, after all, had three women, including Sara herself, to minister to his domestic comforts) and an intensifying physical need for Sara herself, which he tried to sublimate. Despite a growing alienation, however, it came as a considerable shock when wounding words of Wordsworth were reported to him – that he had been an 'absolute nuisance in his household' and that he 'had no hope of him'. Coleridge's reaction is recorded at once in the notebooks: 'Sunday Night. No Hope of me! absol. Nuisance! God's mercy is it a Dream?' and, a day or two later: 'Whirled about without a center – as in a nightmair – no gravity – a vortex without a center.' Moving as these entries are in context, they might still seem an over-reaction to reported remarks by an old friend. To appreciate their full resonance we must look again at what had been happening during the previous decade.

Here again the notebooks bring fresh evidence to bear. In what is a fairly clear reference to himself, Coleridge discusses the condition of a man 'whom a *pernicious Drug* shall make capable of conceiving & bringing forth Thoughts, hidden in him before, which shall call forth the deepest feelings of his best, greatest, & sanest Contemporaries'. One possible explanation for this paradoxical phenomenon, he suggests, is that 'the dire poison for a delusive time has made the body, i.e., the *organization*, not the articulation (or instruments of motion) the unknown somewhat, a fitter Instrument for the all-powerful Soul'.

The implication is significant: that opium had, in the very process of wrecking his health, assisted the emergence of ideas which others, at least, had been able to put to good use. And the supposed beneficiaries must surely include Wordsworth, who had found in Coleridge's ideas an important stimulus for his own productions. His acknowledgment of this evidently acted as a balm to Coleridge's easily-roused sense of guilt; to watch Wordsworth writing his 'Poem to Coleridge' (which we now know as *The Prelude*) through assimilation of Coleridgean ideas to the interpretation of his own experience was to feel that his own failures had not been altogether in vain.

By the same token, Wordsworth's reported comments to a third party had a disproportionately blasting effect, removing at one stroke the sense of fostering loyalty; it was a long time before Coleridge recovered equilibrium. When he did, it was to see his friend with a much colder eye. Now he balanced certain weaknesses against his greatness 'the attorneysonship of the Trismegistus', as he termed them – and allowed himself some bitter comments, voicing a belief that if Wordsworth published his poem he would cancel all the passages relating to Coleridge's philosophy 'as instances of mutual interpenetration of 2 = 1' and even writing a satirical squib (later deleted) about the Wordsworthian relationship of husband, sister and wife.

Throughout the next decade, Coleridge's physical condition continued to deteriorate. By 1820 he could refuse an invitation to dinner on the grounds of 'the sudden seizures to which I am ...most liable after any excitement of animal spirits from genial society'. Nor was it a simple affair of alternating good and bad health; many men have performed their intellectual feats against worse physical odds. Coleridge's problem was that the very animal energies which he could no longer trust had formerly played a key part in his thought. In more hopeful days he had even thought it possible to descry, in their more sensitive workings, the presence of a benevolent world-spirit.

It was precisely because his thought had always included this self-involving element that his physical sufferings rebounded at the intellectual level. Where the free play of his energies had formerly provided cohesive links for his poetry and thought, giving his conversation, poems and best prose a firm current of probing intelligence, severance of those links left him exposed to a division within the registering psyche between the weary, ongoing mechanical movements and needs of his body and the yearning spirit that still looked before and after. The myth of 'The Ancient Mariner' realized itself afresh in his own career, as he found himself becalmed, racked between the death-in-life of his physical burdens and the life-in-death of his persisting imaginative aspirations. The duality between body and soul is a familiar enough literary theme, but here the division cuts differently and is being reported by (to quote Virginia Woolf again) 'a man of exaggerated self-consciousness, endowed with an astonishing power of self-analysis'.

The notebooks expose still further the biographers' Coleridge: a figure who has always attracted unusual sympathy or unusual contempt, according to the presuppositions of the observer. Along with the lovingly described loss of creative power, there is an extraordinary range of achievements: *The Friend, Zapolya, Biographia Literaria, Sibylline Leaves*, the *Lay Sermons*, the various sets of lectures. And if in these we sometimes detect a desperate frame stretched across areas of self-contradiction we may also trace a quality hinted at in Lamb's well-known report: 'He is very bad, but then he wonderfully picks up another day, and his face when he repeats his verses hath its ancient glory ...' These later writings are still haunted by vestiges from the earlier time when his animal spirits were in full play, encouraging him to speculate more readily concerning possible links between the manifestations of life, postulating a God who was in some sense identifiable with 'Nature's vast ever-acting Energy' and writing the poetry of an energized imagination. Even now, anything in German thought or contemporary scientific speculation which might give support to those earlier speculations is seized upon and noted down.

For his more positive philosophy Coleridge takes a line which corresponds more precisely with his growing self-division, but still harks back to an earlier time. If he now speaks up more often in favour of the great religious institutions and of traditional Christianity, it is partly because he sees them as guarding the moral significance of the one form of physical energy that has never betrayed him: light.

Light is a constant, if unobtrusive, presence throughout the later writings, particularly the poetry. Sometimes it comes near to reviving the poetic power of the early Coleridge – as when he describes his glimpse of a hawk defecating in the sunlight:

> The soil that fell from the Hawk poised at the extreme boundary of Sight thro' a column of sunshine – a falling star, a gem, the fixation, & chrystal, of substantial Light, again dissolving & elongating like a liquid Drop – how altogether lovely this to the Eye, and to the Mind too while it remained its own self, all & only its very Self – . What a wretched Frenchman would not he be, who could shout out – charming Hawk's Turd!

For a moment the grossness of the physical universe is transfigured and the aspiring Coleridge set free; yet only to emphasize his central problem: is there or is there not a relationship between the transfiguring power of physical light and the power of human love? The belief that there was had, after all, played a crucial part in his love for Sara, who seemed sometimes to shine with a radiance of her own. The lines which he wrote about this sense of her recur several times in the notebooks:

> All Look or likeness caught from Earth,
> All accident of Kin or Birth,
> Had pass'd away: there was no trace
> Of aught upon her brighten'd face,
> Uprais'd beneath that rifted Stone,
> But of one Image – all her own!
> She, She alone, and only She
> Shone thro' her body visibly.
> (3291)

Even though the love for her which he had based on such experiences had led to emotional disaster, he could not abandon his interest in the mystery involved. His surviving belief that the ability of light to incarnate itself in the flesh might be a key to understanding human experience itself helps to explain much of his later career – including his difficulty in achieving an adequate and free-flowing central language. While he can write with extraordinary facility on many matters, there are some where the available language seems inadequate. Hence, paradoxically, his willingness to appropriate the language of others when it offers an approximation to his own thoughts and sentiments. Those who read him primarily in order to discover his unacknowledged borrowings will find little new material in this volume; they may take solace, however, in a series of notebook entries, collected in good faith by his grandson for *Anima Poetae*, which turn out to have been based largely on prose meditations by J. P. F. Richter – and presumably to have been seized upon by Coleridge to remedy his deficiency in expressing related sentiments. They include a number of notes on the relationship between love and light (including the observation that in Nova Zembla the image of the sun appears on the horizon sixteen days before the sun itself), and an entry which Lowes used as the epigraph for the last section of *The Road to Xanadu*:

> If a man could pass thro' Paradise in a Dream, & have a flower presented to him as a pledge that his Soul had really been there, & found that flower in his hand when he awoke ...(4287)

'how he would yearn for that Elysian land, whenever he looked at the flower', continued Jean Paul lyrically; Coleridge's own yearning poses itself more quizzically: 'Aye! and what then?' he concludes.

It is the riddle that hovers over his whole career, and which he knows to hover as he sits (to quote Shelley's heightened lines),

> obscure
> In the exceeding lustre and the pure
> Intense irradiation of a mind,
> Which, with its own internal lightning blind,
> Flags wearily through darkness and despair ...

These notebooks, more than any other surviving documents, convey both the irradiation and the despair; it is the editor's great achievement to have made them accessible with annotations which illuminate not only the strengths and weaknesses of Coleridge's completed works and lectures of the period but also the period as a whole.

It would be surprising if such copious annotation did not sometimes provoke disagreement. At entry 3672, for instance, the editor, by not recording the underlining of Mary's name when translating the cipher and by ignoring the suggestion of contrast in Coleridge's colon, seems to have been led to treat the personal defects under discussion as referring to both Mary and Sara Hutchinson, rather than to Mary as opposed to Sara. In one or two other cases, obviously, the annotation will be added to over the years.

The presentation, which is otherwise wholly admirable, may be similarly criticized in one or two respects. Unless a note was dated by Coleridge, it is very difficult indeed for a scholar who may be working from manuscripts or from previous transcriptions (such as Anima Poetae) to know where to look for any given passage in this edition as it proceeds. A full key is promised in the final volume, but in the meantime much additional work is created and inaccurate earlier versions are perpetuated. The dating provided in the running headlines, also, is often over-simplified, as reference to the notes or apparatus will show; specific dating of each note in the margin would have been more helpful. Just occasionally, too, the transcription falls below its customary impeccability: a redundant tau has intruded into the Greek at 3421; some superfluous characters have been facsimiled with the cipher at 4032; the proofreading has missed 'underpraved' (for undepraved) at 4033, 'Ismium' (for Osmium) at 4309 and a numeral which should be shown as deleted at 3289. The punctuation (particularly in the verse transcriptions) is sometimes a shade erratic.

These are minimal points, however, worthy of mention only in an edition which prides itself on never needing to use '*sic*', however aberrant the original text. One retires quickly from them to contemplate the magnitude of the achievement – four and a half thousand entries annotated so far – and to ask whether there has been another editing feat of such proportions during the present century.

Once or twice, in spite of everything, the editor is forced to confess herself beaten – and here it is in the spirit of the edition that a reviewer should invite further help. Does any reader know whether it was really Erasmus who used the expression 'ubi non fur, ibi stultus' (4269) – and if so, where? Or where to find the story of the German woman who, falling in love on a sudden presentiment that a certain man would be her husband, had his wife poisoned and then, brought to trial many years later, could say nothing except 'God is Just!' (4275)? Or which Italian writer said that a man who always eats partridge will sometimes crave for the flesh of the starling (3306)?

A COMPENDIUM OF CLICHÉ

THE POET AS ESSAYIST

Coleridge earned some part of his breads, books, and drugs as an essayist and leader-writer for the *Morning Post* and *Courier*, intermittently between 1798 and 1818. In 1850 his daughter Sara identified some of these pieces and collected them in three volumes of *Essays*. The present edition greatly enlarges upon that earlier edition, for the editor, David Erdman, has conclusively identified many more of Coleridge's contributions. The volumes take towards the half-way-mark the editorial venture (the *Collected Works* of Coleridge) which, under the general editorship of Kathleen Coburn, and with the enlightened support of the Bollingen Foundation, has enlisted the services of many excellent scholars. Princeton University Press is to be congratulated on the handsome production.

Congratulation, in fact, should be sent in every direction, except to the author of the *Essays*. I will come to him in due course. But, first, I will depart from the usual convention in reviewing, in which the established author is deferred to over several columns, and the editor is then handed the small change of quibbles. For in this case the editor is the more interesting man of the two. I forget on what occasion, and by whom, David Erdman was found, in the high Cold War, to be un-American. He has probably forgotten also. It was a common visitation at that time upon independence of mind. The universities, in that age of servility, seemed to close against him; he became an un-Professor also. We might have lost a great scholar and editor if that bold 'people's university,' the New York Public Library, had not had the integrity, and also the excellent sense of its own best interests, to secure his services in its department of publications. Here, in the very heart of Manhattan, the conspiracy was hatched, which was destined to undermine reputations, destroy received opinions, and revive forgotten causes. Erdman's memorable study of *Blake: Prophet Against Empire* only initiated a prolonged campaign that reached into the recesses of scholarship in Romantic literature. The Library's Bulletin, under his editorship, enhanced its international reputation. Moreover, being an un-Professor, he somehow emerged unmarked by the professional jealousy that too many academics succumb to.

He is quite the most generous scholar that I have ever known. Some twenty years ago, when I was quite unknown to him, I sent to him an inquiry about some work I was doing (and still am doing) on the Romantic poets in England in the 1790s. There came back across the Atlantic, not only a long, informative letter, but a package of his own research files, which, to my shame, remain still under my hand. As I came to know the (not always-so-fraternal) fraternity of Romantic scholars better, I found that my experience was not exceptional. This may easily be tested. Pick up any serious work on English Romantic literature published in the last two decades, and in two cases out of three you will find Erdman's help acknowledged, often in the warmest terms. A few years ago Erdman slipped back into the academy, at Stony Brook, although he remains an Editor at the Library. So he is now a Professor and (one must suppose) a mellow American, one of the élite in a richly-endowed field of scholarship. His views are now being challenged in their turn, as is proper. But even as they challenge them, the challengers know that they stand on the ground he first cleared and brought under the plough.

And what a clearance is made in these volumes! One admires, first of all, the editor's economy. The editorial introduction, which takes us through Coleridge's murky relations with the newspapers' proprietor, Daniel Stuart, and through the author's crablike political evolutions, is as compressed as anthracite. It demands careful reading. It does not intrude with the editor's opinions; indeed, there is evident self-denial. In one or two earlier volumes of the Bollingen edition we were faced with page upon page of footnotes, appended to a few lines of text. The editor, in one case, thought it necessary to inform his readers as to what a Justice of the Peace was and managed to be both prolix and misleading in the explanation. Erdman's notes are necessary, apt, informed and informative, and precise. If a judgment is called for, it is conveyed by a wry image, by a juxtaposition of two of Coleridge's incompatible sentiments, or by the mere suggestion of the raising of an editorial eyebrow.

As to Coleridge's fully recovered texts, I must say that my own eyebrows shot up early in Volume I and did not descend until Volume III was closed. These books are most damaging to Coleridge's reputation as an exalted political thinker, and, moreover, it is altogether proper that this inflated reputation should be so damaged. The ingredients of Coleridge's political thought – historical, philosophical – were exceptionally rich, but the results were always half-baked. In the early 1790s he allowed his friends, his colleagues, and his wife, to suppose that he was an ultra-Jacobin, who disdained mere political equality because he espoused social equality, a kind of communist 'aspheterism.' He dreamed up a 'practical' (and preposterous) scheme of Pantisocracy, to be founded on the banks of the Susquehanna.

For some of Coleridge's radical contemporaries, who followed Dr. Joseph Priestley into exile at his extensive land purchases around Forksville, Pennsylvania, this was an earnest and practicable venture. Their plots are registered in the Land Office at Harrisburg under such names as 'Hope,' 'Fortitude,' 'Liberty' and 'Utopia.' For Coleridge the scheme led no further than into a row with his brother-in-law, Robert Southey. Coleridge was, in those days, highly enlightened as to women's rights. The women 'can at least prepare the Food of Simplicity for us – let the married Women do only what is absolutely convenient and customary for pregnant Women or nurses – Let the Husbands do *all* the Rest – and what will that all be -? Washing with a Machine and cleaning the House. One Hour's addition to our daily Labour – and Pantisocracy in it's most perfect Sense is practiable' (*Letters*, ed. E. L. Griggs [1956-71], I, 114). But the women, nevertheless, were thought to be a liability. Did they have, he asked Southey, 'the generous enthusiasm of Benevolence,' or merely an excitement at the novelty of the scheme? Were their minds properly saturated with 'the Divinity of Truth'? If not, then the women would bring an infection into the heart of Eden; they would 'tinge the Mind of the Infants with prejudications' (*Letters*, I, 119).

That is an immense age (a full four years) before these volumes open; but at no point, in more than one thousand pages, does it occur to Coleridge to doubt that his *own* mind is saturated with the Divinity of Truth. I find these essays objectionable, not on account of their opinions – although most of these are lamentable – but on account of the unction with which they are delivered. Whatever prejudice Coleridge chooses to announce, it is first mounted on exalted moral stilts. He alone writes from Principle, and hence his views are 'sanctified' (a favourite word). Whole essays are given over to sanctimonious strategies designed to exhibit his own moral probity, his consistency, and to abuse the motives attributed to his opponents who were often his former colleagues or friends (Dyer, Thelwall, Gilbert Wakefield, William Frend, Godwin), who faced the threat of imprisonment and the attentions of the various un-British-Activities organs of that time, and who had little opportunity to answer back.

As we enter the essays, in 1798, Coleridge is still a man of the Left (an advocate of Peace), although preparing his evacuation. The evacuation is made by way of a prolonged critique of Buonaparte and of the betrayal by revolutionaries of the principles behind the French Revolution. The 'character and conduct of Napoleon' (Sara Coleridge noted) was 'the plank or bridge' whereby her father passed over 'from warm interest in the cause of the French nation to decided Anti-Gallicanism,' from advocacy of peace to the most bellicose advocacy of war. Erdman adds that in the *Morning Post* essays 'we see Coleridge frequently on that plank or bridge, running back and forth or pausing uncertainly in the middle' (I, lxiv). These early essays are undoubtedly the most interesting; they provide evidence of an inflamed political sensibility, a tormented inner argument, and, with all the abhorrence of Napoleon's measures, a just appreciation of his active genius. Thereafter a shutter seems to close in Coleridge's mind. The matter is settled. If inner argument persists, it is severely repressed. Arguments give way to imprecations; the French are governed by 'Liberticides,' who have 'no voice but to utter brothelry and blasphemy;' the cause lies in part in French national character ('this vain, yet shallow, this frivolous, yet ferocious race'), but, above all, in the False Philosophy of Jacobinism – the ungodly and vicious illusion of equality of natural rights.

As one lays the volumes down one is sickened by the surfeit of pharisaism and cliché. Coleridge is always writing 'from my inmost soul,' he offers himself as 'a teacher of moral wisdom.' But the content of this wisdom might be better entitled 'Coleridge's Compendium of Cliché.' We move among Molochs, pilots in stormy seas, and engineers sapping the earth with Jacobin mines; bones lie bleaching everywhere; we move among volcanoes, avalanches and earthquakes; we admire palladiums of humanity and England's 'gracious line of Kings;' we learn of the 'natural good sense of Britons,' of voices 'from the sepulchres of our forefathers,' of 'man, the superior being, the protector of the other sex,' and of the middle class as the 'greatest blessing and ornament of human nature.' And so on, and on. When, at the end of the Wars, the popular movement for Reform erupts, Coleridge is terrified by the spectre of Jacobinism revived. But he thinks the demands of argument (and of Philosophy) are met by characterizing working-class reformers as 'malcontents and potwise senators of ale-houses,' and assuming them to be 'fanatic or dissolute.'

This is serious; and it should be serious to Coleridge's reputation. Some part of his contributions to the *Courier* are no more than the occasional productions of the political journalist; he was a kind of Mr. William Safire of that time, and his work should be given as little, or as much, attention as this merits. But in other parts he assumed an altogether more exalted and prophetic character; he struggled to imitate the orotund periods and elevated jeremiads of Burke in his last writings, just as he borrowed from Burke the only consistent ideas (as to property and duty) to be found in these pages. For too long scholars have been found to take him at his own evaluation. Because Coleridge wrote several great poems (mostly before 1800), because he was immensely erudite and had a richly jumbled mind and an exuberant fertility of invention – to be seen always at its best in unfinished artifacts, that is, in conversation, letters and notebooks – because of all these, many have assumed that all he did must have been great, and that his most rotund clichés must be profound.

They were not. The more he tried to work up his impulses into finished thoughts, the more unprincipled he became. He is chiefly of interest, in his political writings, as an example of the intellectual complexity of apostasy. He was, of course, a political apostate, and critics have confused the matter only because they have removed it from a political to an aesthetic court of judgment. A literary critic can afford to be tolerant towards a writer if he strikes good images – and ambiguity can be a literary virtue. But there are, after all, other grounds of judgment.

If a political writer takes up an exposed and unpopular position, then he has some obligation to defend his fellow-exposed, even if they are making fools of themselves (as they generally are). If he arrives at the conclusion that he has been utterly mistaken, and on fundamental points, then two reputable courses would seem to be open to him. One is the difficult course of arguing the matter through, without caricaturing one's past allegiances or allies or manipulating evidence. This is what Wordsworth did, over a period of eight years, in writing the *Prelude*. The other is a little interval for silence and self-criticism. But Coleridge swung instantly to the most bitter attacks, accompanied by malicious imputations as to the motives of his friends and extended manipulations of his own autobiography, in order to pillory positions that all supposed to have been his own. He was, in any political judgment, disloyal, egocentric, and wholly irresponsible. There was also a dash of the Whittaker Chambers about him. Whatever auto-suppression of his impulses went on in these years, the evidence survives here in the rawness, the malevolence and utter lack of generosity of his denunciation of those who held to positions that had once been his own.

The danger of these kinds of people has become known in our time. The Congress for Cultural Freedom had one or two pocket-Coleridges in its midst. But what next alarms is

Coleridge's exemplification of the utter irresponsibility of a certain kind of intellectual with pretentions to political authority. Throughout these twenty years, Coleridge was wrong on almost everything, except in his prescience as to Napoleon's genius and lasting powers. But he had to take none of the consequences that humbler political mortals must take. During the brief Peace of Amiens, as leader-writer in an influential daily, he helped to lash the country back to war; then he retired back to his 'old folios' and the peaceful scenes of the Lake District. Principle had been vindicated!

Examine his record on the question of Ireland. One of the most tragic consequences of the Wars is to be found in the savage repression of the rebellion of 1798, the ensuing political segregation of Catholic and Protestant Ireland (for the United Irishmen had owed as much to the 'Jacobin' national consciousness of Wolfe Tone and Emmett in the Protestant North as to the Catholic peasantry of Wexford), and the enforced dissolution of an Irish Parliament in the subject 'Union' with Britain. And what do we find, on all this, from our brilliant essayist's pen? First of all, silence, at any point after the rebellion, as to the extreme savagery with which it was put down. Page upon page on Buonaparte's military crimes: not one word on Castlereagh's. It is true that there is once a suggestion that he *would* make some protest if it were 'safe', which it was not; as Erdman reminds us, other journalists had been imprisoned for doing so. The Irish are characterized as 'a wild and barbarous race' (I, 106); called to account, Coleridge pretends to apologize, but slips in the phrase 'the ferocious vindictiveness of savage tribes.' Then Coleridge supports the Act of Union (1800) and comes forward as an opponent of Catholic Emancipation (1811); Ireland cannot be trusted, being 'in the last and lowest rank of the civilized world' (II, 281). Then, in 1814, Coleridge unleashes eight virulent and totally uninformed attacks upon an Irish judge, Mr. Justice Fletcher, who, in a charge of grave and measured humanity, had appealed for conciliation, had reprimanded English alarmists (such as Coleridge), and had dared to mention injustices against Catholic Irish perpetrated by the (technically illegal but openly condoned) Orange Lodges. It is an ignorant and vicious attack, and, so far as I know, Professor Erdman is the first scholar who has bothered to dig out Fletcher's humane charge and allow the reader to judge Coleridge's credibility.

Thus Coleridge was an active agent in enforcing that alienation of two cultures that has brought us, directly, to the present day. I do not say this because I am a supporter of the Provisional I.R.A., as to whom there continue to be the most sentimental illusions. A United Ireland will not come without some rediscovery of the spirit and aims of the United Irishmen, and that must include the national aspirations (of Tone and Emmett) of the North. But Coleridge helped to prepare the ground, and to get ready the guns, for today's exercises. His 'wisdom' in this was one of the influences he transmitted to Thomas Carlyle, another Hibernian hater. Surely all these 'great men' are not to be excused from the responsibilities of common mortals just because they were 'great'?

Coleridge found national sentiment and patriotism to be wholly moral and sanctified wherever it related to the British. It was despicable only when found in the Irish or the French. Erdman does not allow the careful reader to be fooled. In one sly footnote he even allows himself the extreme license of criticizing, by implication, Kathleen Coburn herself. For she has written, in a learned article, that 'politically [Coleridge] came to believe in an enlightened but expansionist colonial policy for Britain, based on the economic and cultural development of territories colonized' (I, cxxvi). This sounds very grand and reputable in a 'great' thinker; but, of course, it means no more than that Coleridge shared in the general rhetoric and claptrap of the commercial imperialism of his time; for what imperialist has ever disclaimed culture and enlightenment, or avowed that it was his intention to rob?

These articles then are, in the main, both irresponsible and unprincipled. For whatever high moral principle Coleridge adduces, the conclusion is reached in terms of British expediency, the nobility of British intentions and arms entailing the nobility of the expedients. They are also badly written. There are, to be sure, here and there, some passages that will afford comfort to the liberals. Coleridge, in one column, expressed himself in severe terms in opposition to the practice of publicly whipping naked women for pilfering. This was enlightened in him. But the close reader of Erdman's notes will be reminded of the actual occasion for this solitary intervention. The opposition press, the enemies of the *Courier*, had been vigorously campaigning against the flogging (sometimes to death) of soldiers (II, 140). Coleridge was trying to draw the scent off the fox. Cobbett was imprisoned for his part in that campaign. Coleridge received two guineas for his.

Well, then, were Coleridge's essays influential? The author was in no doubt; he was always building fantasies, in which his essays were 'sensations' and in which the Ministers, who never bothered to make his acquaintance, were guided by him in their deliberations. As to this, there is no confirming evidence. There is, perhaps, one place where his influence might be surmised. Throughout 1811, Coleridge was writing a series of splenetic, but highly moralistic, paragraphs advocating the assassination of Buonaparte. Tyrannicide was justified, but only in extreme circumstances, which Coleridge could identify. As it happens, Buonaparte was not assassinated. But, next year, the Prime Minister of Great Britain, Spencer Perceval, was. If any of Coleridge's incitements to tyrannicide had lodged in the disturbed mind of the assassin, John Bellingham, then at last Coleridge's sentiments had winged a palpable object. After all, if Coleridge could identify the circumstances that justified this measure, why could not Bellingham also? Such is the common outcome of inflammatory moral rhetoric in the service of expediency.

In fact, Coleridge's serviceability to the *Post* and the *Courier* was simpler than that. It could be seen at a glance that he was a man whose vanity allowed him to be easily led. Erdman speculates too little upon the motives of the newspapers' proprietor, Daniel Stuart. His main motive was probably that of making money, sometimes (by imposing forged news upon the stocks) by illegal means. But he also wished both to keep in with Ministers and to keep circulation up by an assumed 'independence.' For this purpose Coleridge, with his reputation as a man of the Left, served as an admirable screen. He could write essay upon essay that supported, in the main points, established power and policy, but that were salted with scruples and luminous ambiguities preserving the pretense of manly independence. Coleridge never used his opportunities in the national press; he was always *used*. The later stages on the *Courier* were more disgraceful. Stuart had lost interest, and the managing editor of the paper, Street, was in receipt of Treasury pay, and was generally known to be so. Coleridge allowed himself to be turned on and off like a tap. He needed the money. When the tap was turned on, and he poured out his abuse at Judge Fletcher or his justification of Old Corruption, all that he did was to comfort mean-minded and self-interested readers with the notion that their interests were sanctified, by a great intellectual, for exalted, if obscure, and principled, if ambiguous, reasons.

In his last years (which lie outside these books) Coleridge

took fright at Utilitarianism; and his subsequent critique of this has more weight, more originality, more interest, and more influence. But the 'thought' of this period is a disaster. I am reporting my own judgment, and not that of Professor Erdman. In the minutiae of his excellent scholarship he has come to love the work so much that he may almost have persuaded himself that the work is worthy of the task. But the editorial work is worthier than its object.

Erdman will, I suppose, not like it when I say that Hazlitt was immeasurably greater than Coleridge as a political thinker and essayist. He was also immeasurably more generous. One of the most interesting aspects of these volumes is that they illustrate the extreme provocation that Coleridge's former friends of the Left were under: Hazlitt, Lamb, Thelwall and others. They also reveal the reasons why the younger 'Left' of the next generation, the Hunts, Keats, Shelley, felt such contempt for their forebears. Coleridge was an apostate, with a voracious appetite for hatreds. Scan these essays, and his letters, and you will scarcely find a generous syllable expressed towards the friends of his Jacobin youth. Hazlitt and his circle, by contrast, hit back in public only when it became publicly essential to do so. They were constrained, not by cowardice, but by a sense of Coleridge's *pathos*: the ruin of a supremely rich but disorderly mind.

Again and again, one has to return to Hazlitt if one wishes to regain a sense of Coleridge's power, if one wishes to find clues to explain the contrast between the attribution to him of 'genius' and the pitiful and sometimes smelly fruits produced. In his study in *The Spirit of the Age*, in 'Consistency of Opinion,' and, above all, in that extraordinarily generous 'My First Acquaintance with Poets' – which recovers the whole exuberant *promise* of young Coleridge, and which turns away the rancor of the years with a slight, melancholy smile – Hazlitt discloses where that genius was lodged. It was always just at the other side of the threshold of execution; it can be seen in the brilliant and contradictory unfashioned materials of his letters and notebooks; it came across the threshold in a few poems, in some criticism, in occasional passages of his other writings. And we understand, from Hazlitt and from Lamb, the gentleness with which the canting editorialist of the *Courier* was handled. Too many were aware of his private infirmities and of the appalling wreck of his genius to see him as anything but a tragic figure.

Editors should continue to handle Coleridge with the same delicacy, as Erdman does. I see less reason to be forgiving since it was decided, in the high Cold War, and sometimes by writers undergoing a similar interior redecoration, that Coleridge was a great and important political thinker. This was always a case of misrecognition, sometimes enacted in front of a mirror. Erdman himself offers no verdict. But his scholarship does, and the imposture of this 'thought' cannot survive the scrutiny of the editor's footnotes.

I find an irony somewhere in this. An editor, a one-time victim of one Cold War, who has kept watch with a calm and equable eye over the scene changes of principle and the involutions of apostasy, has at last brought to book the spurious rhetoric of a chameleon from a comparable age. Erdman is also a better prose writer than Coleridge, when he makes the attempt. His images have more felicity. As he says, of one series of warmongering letters addressed by Coleridge to Fox, these 'are but fungi springing from the dark hints of Stuart's [the newspaper proprietor's] own paragraphs' (I, 388n).

HUNTING THE JACOBIN FOX

> ... proscribed and hunted – driven like a wild beast, and banished, like a contagion, from society ...he was chased like a worse than outlaw ...[1]

I. VIEW HALLOO!

How far did a 'loyal' consensus reign in England in the last years of the 1790s?[2] How far were members of the middle classes disaffected? Who were the 'Jacobins'? How are we to read the experience of political defeat and intellectual retreat among the active reformers? We may take John Thelwall as an exemplar.

There has recently been renewed interest in the political writings of Thelwall in the earlier 1790s. He was driven out of public life in Britain in 1797-8. His defeat coincided with the 'annus mirabilis' of Wordsworth and Coleridge's *Lyrical Ballads*, and Thelwall was known to the poets. He was a survivor of the notorious treason trials of 1794, and whereas his fellow victims (or 'acquitted felons' as William Windham called them)[3] – Thomas Hardy and John Horne Tooke – kept their distance from prominent public activity in association with advanced reformers, Thelwall resumed a very prominent public role as a lecturer and in the councils of the London Corresponding Society.[4] His lectures, delivered in Beaufort Buildings off the Strand, were published in his periodical, the

Tribune. It is clear that Thelwall was looking to a more up-market audience than that usually to be found in a division of the Corresponding Society. He had always been ambitious to cut a figure in the world of letters, and he had published several volumes of poetry, including *The Peripatetic* (1793). His lectures in the Beaufort Buildings enlisted audiences of from four hundred to five hundred, who were charged the comparatively high entrance fee of one shilling or sixpence, and he claimed that even 'aristocrats' thronged to hear him.[5] From 1795 to 1797 were high-tide years for Godwinian enthusiasm and the same rising of middle-class enthusiasm gave buoyancy to Thelwall.

The story of the silencing of Thelwall should commence with the passage of the Two Acts in November 1795. These included clauses specifically designed to prohibit political lectures. Thelwall not unreasonably concluded that these were aimed at him, and he circumvented the Acts by renewing lectures under the disguise of disquisitions of 'Roman history'.[6]

For reasons that are not wholly clear he left London in the summer of 1796 and extended his mission to Norwich.[7] While he might talk freely about political questions at small house meetings, any such meeting of above forty-nine persons was controlled under the Two Acts. Therefore (once again) he delivered a course of twenty-two lectures on 'Classical History, and particularly the Laws and Revolutions of Rome'.[8] Norwich was a strong reform centre, both middle-class and plebeian, and the lectures passed off without incident and without challenge at law.

Thelwall enjoyed the 'intercourse of a most agreeable and intelligent circle of society',[9] which included some of those who, in the previous year, had gathered around a Norwich journal of philosophic radicalism, the *Cabinet*. Anne Plumptre, like her sister, a writer, was 'charmed' with Thelwall:

> Words cannot express how much charmed, as an orator he is wonderful, as a man even more to be admired, – stern only in his adherence to virtue. His manners have an enchanting urbanity in them, which renders him no less delightful in private society, than his transcendent powers of oratory render him in the tribune.[10]

We should note that there were many women among his audiences, in London, Norwich and Yarmouth.[11] But not all of his hearers were so charmed. The young Crabb Robinson found 'his address was full of catch claps'. His friend Thomas Amyot was 'frequently pleased by his ingenuity & lively sallies, tho sometimes disgusted by his sophistry & traps for vulgar applause'.[12] In less favourable mood he reported that: 'He raves like a mad Methodist parson: the most ranting Actor in the most ranting Character never made so much noise as Citizen Thelwall ...'[13]

It is true that Thelwall's oratory was histrionic, and one may get little idea from the printed record of the tricks of rhetoric and performance to which he had recourse. Almost certainly it was of Thelwall that William Hazlitt wrote in the *Plain Speaker*:

> The most dashing orator I ever heard is the flattest writer I ever read. In speaking, he was like a volcano vomiting out *lava*; in writing, he is like a volcano burnt out ...He was the model of a flashy, powerful demagogue... He was possessed, infuriated with the patriotic *mania*; he seemed to rend and tear the rotten carcase of corruption ...The lightning of national indignation flashed from his eye; the working of the popular mind were seen labouring in his bosom ...but ...read one of these very popular and electrical effusions ...and you would not believe it to be the same![14]

He preferred to strike a theatrical posture in which he on his own was challenging the whole state, and he clearly enjoyed his notorious defiance of the Two Acts. He could even sacrifice his own children to enliven his rhetoric. In a lecture while the Two Acts were passing he declared:

> I am not very careful, citizens, about my words tonight: for I declare no death is so terrible to me as living to see the day in which the bill is accepted. I have two infants, the joy of a father's heart, whose innocent smiles furnish my only relaxation ...But I protest sooner would I see those infants strangled before my face, sooner would I have my body pierced through like a culender ...than live under the reproach of suffering this bill to pass without all the opposition I have the power of making ...[15]

No wonder that Southey in later years called Thelwall 'a consummate coxcomb'; but he also said, 'He is a good-hearted man; besides, we ought never to forget that he was once as near as possible being hanged, and there is great merit in that'.[16] Thelwall himself was not likely to allow his auditors to forget this 'merit', which contributed so largely to his fame.

The Norwich lectures were interrupted by the general election, when Thelwall withdrew for three weeks to Westminster to help his fellow 'felon', John Horne Tooke (who was not elected). In Norwich the city was in a state of electoral excitement. The reformers found an unenthusiastic candidate in the person of Bartlet Gurney, a wealthy Quaker who was believed to favour universal manhood suffrage and who was willing to allow his name to go forward against William Windham, the War Minister, but who took no part in the campaign: the reformers' slogan was 'Peace and Gurney – No More War – No More Barley Bread'. In the result the sitting candidate, Henry Hobart (1622) was returned, and also Windham (1159), with Gurney a close runner-up (1076). The margin between Windham and Gurney could be more than accounted for by out-voters for Windham imported for the occasion. Anne Plumptre wrote indignantly that 'the crew who have elected Windham are as a drop in a bucket compared with the whole population of the town, and they have brought him in amidst the execrations of the rest of their fellow-Citizens'.[17]

On Thelwall's return to the city a significant reconciliation took place between the philosophical and the more activist tendencies among the 'Jacobins'. William Godwin and Thelwall had fallen out in the run-up to the passage of the Two Acts. Godwin had published a pamphlet which seemed to condone the government's suppression of inflammatory lectures, and which compared Thelwall's professions of his peaceable intent to Iago's conduct, who, when he had done all in his power to arouse Othello's suspicions, counselled him 'not to give harbour to a thought of jealousy'.[18] In response Thelwall gibed (with some justice) that Godwin proposed that the public mind was to be transformed 'by writing quarto volumes, and conversing with a few speculative philosophers by the fire side'.[19] Robinson's cynical friend Thomas Amyot witnessed the reconciliations:

> GODWIN while at Norwich was reconciled to Thelwall at William Taylor's & I have since seen them walking together round our Castle Hill. Of course the former will no longer be accused of 'cherishing a feebleness of spirit', nor will the latter be again compared to Iago. Like Gog & Magog …they will now go hand in hand in their glorious schemes.[20]

It was against this background that Thelwall acceded to a strong request from Great Yarmouth to deliver six lectures there. The authorities were perhaps alarmed by the success of his Norwich lectures, an alarm which might have been heightened by Windham's narrow victory in the election. At any rate the story was put about that Thelwall was raising the provinces to revolt:

160

When Thelwall, for the season, quits the Strand
To organize revolt by sea and land.[21]

Full accounts survive of the Yarmouth events so that we
may examine this manifestation of loyalism quite closely.[22] As
in Norwich Thelwall had political discussions at two meetings
with less than forty-nine persons, and as at Norwich some of
the 'principal inhabitants' and members of 'decent substantial
families', women as well as men, came to his support.[23] The
lectures were in an exposed position in a hall on the seafront,
and were attended by some two hundred persons of both sexes,
including a few children. At the first two lectures the hall was
surrounded by a parcel of yobbos 'instigated by a Naval
Officer' to pull down the house, but no serious incident took
place.[24] On the third night about ninety sailors armed with
bludgeons burst in upon the audience and laid about them on
all sides They were marshalled by Captain Roberts of the
naval sloop, L'Espiegle, and another officer of the same ship,
both armed with cutlasses. Thelwall attempted to make his
escape, was seized at the door, was rescued by some friends,
and (not without presenting a pistol at an assailant) made his
get-away to a house which the crowd later threatened to pull
down. (This was prevented by the signal guns which called all
hands back on board.) Several of the auditors were seriously
injured and the victors carried trophies, including shawls,
bonnets, wigs, shoes, hats, coats and Thelwall's books, back to
their ships.[25] To the honour of Thelwall and the Yarmouth
reformers, the three remaining lectures were safely delivered.

Depositions in the Court of King's Bench fill in the
details. By chance a blind fiddler and his sighted son were on
board L'Espiegle during the week of the affair, and they were
willing to give evidence. On the day of the affray Captain
Roberts came on board and mustered all hands. He selected
thirty-six of them, told them to take sticks and 'go on shore to

take the preacher ...and bring him on board'. They were not to pull down the house but to 'go in and play at single Stick'. According to other deponents this party was joined on shore by sailors from other men-of-war. Before the hall was broken into, an officer drew the men up and said 'Come my brave Boys let's sing God save the King', and this was followed by three cheers. After the audience had been assaulted and dispersed, a ship's lieutenant said 'My lads demolish every thing and leave nothing standing', and the chairs and all the furniture were promptly smashed. On board *L'Espiegle* the fiddler and his son witnessed the men return, bearing their trophies. One of the seamen said he 'had got some of the Bougre's books and another that there was a Bloody Bougre with a Bald Pate upstairs [in the Gallery] whome they threw down and basted well'. (Perhaps this was the stout gentleman who reeled out of the hall covered in blood and who exclaimed 'Sure I cannot be in a Christian Country'.) No doubt this loyal demonstration may also be seen as contributing to the 'apotheosis of George III'.[26]

It is clear from both loyalist and reformist sources that the intention of this affair was to kidnap Thelwall, take him on board and impress him.[27] In which case the marauders had bungled. It is testimony to Thelwall's courage and sense of political duty that he accepted further invitations to lecture at two other seaports, King's Lynn and Wisbech. At Lynn a large number of merchant seamen created a disturbance outside the hall, supported by a press gang. Some forced themselves into the lecture-room and called for 'Good save the king', but were driven out by the audience. The rioters contented themselves with breaking the windows. The next two (and final) lectures at Lynn were invested in a similar way, and were defended from invasion by the audience. Thelwall then went on to Wisbech, where he was welcomed by placards invoking another verse of 'God save the king':

O lord our God arise, scatter our Enemies,
And make them fall
Confound their politics, frustrate their knavish tricks,
On thee our hopes we fix,
God save us all.

Here his lecture was attended by a 'rough music' led by a detachment of the military. In all three towns the magistracy was applied to for protection, without avail.

Several historians have been kind enough to advise us that Pitt's measures against reformers fell far short of a White Terror. We may thank them for disclosing this hitherto undetected truth: no guillotine was set up at Tyburn. But the Britain of 1796-7, when the 'anarchic cry' went up of 'No Law for Jacobins!',[28] could be an uncomfortable place for reformers. Thelwall, who was one of the few who tried to straddle the world of letters and that of popular agitation,[29] occasionally came to the notice of the *Anti-Jacobin*:

Thelwall's my man for State Alarm:
I love the Rebels of Chalk Farm;
Rogues that no Statues can subdue,
Who'd bring the French, and head them too.[30]

More than twenty years later, during the renewed post-war agitations for reform, Thelwall was to emerge from political retirement, set up his own journal – the *Champion* – and offer himself once more in a leading role. This was resented by some reformers, who chided him for having deserted the cause in the interval.[31] Thelwall was enraged, and responded with an account of his persecutions in those years, when he was:

proscribed and hunted – driven like a wild beast, and banished, like a contagion, from society – during those reiterated attempts by armed banditti, to kidnap and to murder him, ...during all those monstrous atrocities at Yarmouth, at Lynn, at Wisbeach, at Derby, on the borders of Leicestershire – at Stockport, and at Norwich …He never did desert the public – the public deserted him.[32]

Several of these incidents may be identified more clearly. Passing through Ashby de la Zouch on private business 'a mob of soldiers and loose people was hired, by certain zealots in that town, to assail him'. It seems that these pursued him as far as Mountsorrel, some fifteen miles. He was eventually rescued by 'an honest Constable of that place (neither a Tory nor a Whig, but a good staunch Reformer) [who] called up a posse to protect him out of town'.[33] At Derby, in March 1797, when Thelwall was lecturing in the Baptist chapel, a crowd outside 'rough musicked' them with drums, horns and hubbub, then broke the windows and threw bricks and stones inside. 'Thelwall, with a pistol in his hand, declared he would shoot any person who molested him, in consequence of which he was suffered to depart.'[34] At Stockport the Volunteers threatened to throw Thelwall into the canal. By his own account he 'planted his back against a wall, pistol in hand', and 'resolved to sell his life dearly', but he was rescued by a friend, and together they 'forced their way through that "most valiant and most loyal corps" '.[35] Most saddening of all, when Thelwall returned to his beloved Norwich at the end of May 1797 the reformers were unable to protect him, and meetings in several inns were broken up by the Inniskilling Dragoons.[36]

Three comments may arise from these affairs. First, a general signal (or wink) seems to have gone around instructing loyalists that Thelwall might be harassed with impunity. Secondly, 'Church and King' and Anti-Jacobin loyalists were turning, as they had done in the 'Priestley riots' in Birmingham[37] and in the subsequent rage for Tom Paine effigy burnings, the symbolic vocabulary and ritual performances of 'rough music' to their own account.[38] Indeed there was a contest in some places to enlist the crowd and command the streets. The same vocabulary was employed by reformers in their centres of strength, such as Sheffield and also Rochester, whose bishop was reported to have said in a Lords' debate that 'the mass of the People had nothing to do with the Laws but to obey them', and in consequence his effigy was ridden on an ass through the streets and then burned.[39] Charles James Fox complained that 'the unfortunate animal, which was of the same name, was condemned to suffer' – presumably foxes also were impaled or burned. The fox, pursued by the hunt – many of whose members we may presume were Volunteers on exercise – also received for this reason the name of 'Charlie', which it bears among huntsmen and women to this day.[40]

The third – and self-evident – consideration is that, however much Thelwall was pursued like a fox, the pursuit stopped short of the kill. Both at that time and later Thelwall travelled many miles on foot and on horse, alone or with one companion, meeting with no hostility (unless provoked by some person in uniform or in authority), and if there had been an intention of assassinating him then the authorities would stand indicted of gross incompetence. The intention was to drive him out of the reform business.

In this it succeeded. For when Thelwall set off, on 29 June 1797, intrepidly, on a long 'pedestrian tour' from London to the West of England and Wales, he already had some vague idea of trying to find a suitable retreat. His wife and family remained in Derby, whither he had moved with them a few weeks before, at the invitation of the proprietors to conduct the local *Courier*. But 'the vehemence of hostility with which that paper was assailed' forced Thelwall out of the office.[41] He had been forced to give up the tenancy of his London home and lecture-hall by mounting debts.[42] He was fed up with the gossip and disputes among the London reformers, and he wrote grumpily to Thomas Hardy, who continued to give aid and advice from the background.

> Do the people of London talk of me at all – what is the lie of the day? (that I am at Portsmouth[43] I have heard already) – but am I gone over to France on a treasonable embassy? am I teaching the United Irishmen the use of Arms? (the great Gun, you know, I learnt to work in the Tower!!!)[44] or have I got a pension for preaching moderation? – or a snug sinecure for arguing against petitions for peace and removal of ministers? or finally have I retired upon an immense fortune collected in crooked sixpences during seven months lectures at Beaufort Buildings? – Something or other I hope and trust the Londoners continue to say about me – & if my enemies cannot invent a lie malignant enough, let them go to my friends and they will help them out.

> Adieu, brother of my political heart – Thou man of plain integrity & inflexible soul I hail thee.[45]

The letter illustrates well another characteristic of movements suffering from repression and dwindling support – the growth of divisions, factionalism and personal animosities.[46] Thelwall may also have had tactical reasons for wishing to distance himself from activists, at a time of naval mutinies, rising disorder in Ireland, gathering invasion threat, and the resort of some members of the London Corresponding Society to treasonable underground activities with the 'United men'.

Thelwall gave none of these reasons for his pedestrian tour. He professed that 'the general aspect of affairs having at length determined him to retire from public exertion' he had resumed his old enthusiasm for 'the picturesque and romantic', and also decided to record 'Every fact connected with the history and actual condition of the labourious classes'. Another motive was to visit on the Somersetshire coast 'an invaluable friend, well known in the literary world', whom as yet he had never seen but with whom he had engaged in a 'familiar and confidential correspondence'.[47] This was of course Samuel Taylor Coleridge, who had also stood out against the Two Acts with his 'theological lectures' in Bristol and with his journal, the *Watchman*.[48]

Thelwall's pedestrian tour is unremarkable, being largely devoted to conventional rehearsals of the 'romantic and picturesque'. He collected a few details of wages and conditions, but his attempts to discover the views of the labouring classes were less happy. That the Jacobin orator was far from transcending the condescending conventions of class is evidenced by a passage a year before in his *Tribune*:

> I have been rambling, according to my wonted practice, in the true democratic way, on foot, from village to village ...I have dropped, occasionally, into the little hedge ale-houses to refresh myself. I have sat down among the rough clowns, whose tattered garments were soiled with their rustic labours; for I have not forgot that all mankind are equally my brethren; and I love to see the labourer in his ragged coat – that is I love the labourer: I am sorry his coat is obliged to be so ragged. I love the labourer then, in his ragged coat, as well as I love the Peer in his ermine; perhaps better ...[49]

As well as this posture may have gone down in Beaufort Buildings it got him less far in the labouring countryside. When he endeavoured to procure information on 'the condition of the labouring poor' from an old thresher at work in a barn, 'Every question was repelled by some sly rub, or sagacious hint; and his arch gestures, and emphatic half-syllables, displayed the self-congratulating cunning of suspicion'. Elsewhere he also encountered the 'jealous reluctance of communication'. Eventually he met with a labourer who was 'inquisitive, shrewd, and communicative'. He claimed to read several newspapers, and was, no doubt, the 'oracle of every pot-house':

Unfortunately, however, we could no way turn his conversation into the channel we desired. He talked of nothing but Parker and the delegates, of war and of parties. In short, he was too full of liquor and *temporary politics*, to furnish any information on the subject of *political economy* ...[50]

This turn to political economy had been preoccupying Thelwall for a year or more. It was signalled in his booklet, *The Rights of Nature* (1796), which reveals a shift from political and constitutional to economic and historical analysis, and which is regarded as his most original contribution to political thought.[51] This was also Thelwall's own opinion. He wrote to his friend Wimpory, in February 1797, that the second part of *The Rights of Nature*:

> is as superior to the first as the noontide sun to the twinkling of a stinking mackerel in the dark. It is the uniform opinion of all the literary men whose judgments I have been able to collect (& their opinion in this respect perfectly agrees with mine) that the 1st is a very indifferent pamphlet – but that the second is very superior to any thing I ever produced before. And one in particular – I mean Coleridge, who tho' a young man is one of the most extraordinary Geniuses & finest scholars of the age does not scruple to pronounce it 'the best pamphlet that has been written since the commencement of the war'.[52]

A projected conclusion to the *Rights of Nature* was never written: it could hardly be done by a fox on the run.

As Thelwall proceeded on his pedestrian excursion his attitude was ambivalent. His travel was becoming known, and he was welcomed by reformers and sometimes requested to hold small meetings: Salisbury, Frome (a 'sad den of Jacobins' where he sold £5 or £6 worth of his publications), Bath, and Bristol, to which he promised to return.[53] He clearly enjoyed the support he met with and felt the temptation of being drawn back into political currency. But early in the tour he recorded that he and his companion 'lamented the condition of our fellow-beings, and formed Utopian plans of retirement and colonisations'.[54] These plans assumed a more urgent and almost-practical aspect when Thelwall reached his first objective, Coleridge at Stowey, and visited William and Dorothy Wordsworth at Alfoxden House, where they had settled only a couple of weeks before.

The episode of Thelwall's visit to the poets, where they were also watched by the government spy, Walsh, has been told so often that it scarcely needs rehearsing once more.[55] Thelwall's letter to Stella, his wife, is saturated with his sense of release from tension, and of relaxation in a retreat both physical and mental. With Wordsworth and Coleridge 'we have been having a delightful ramble today among the plantations of a wild romantic dell ...through which a foaming, murmuring, rushing torrent of water winds its long artless course'. 'There have we sometimes sitting on a tree – sometimes wading boottop deep thro the stream & again stretched on some mossy stone, a literary & political triumvirate passed sentence on the productions and characters of the age.' Here they 'philosophised [their] minds into a state of tranquillity which the leaders of nations might envy and the residents of Cities can never know'. Thelwall could not yet say 'how many days I may loose the world in this scene of enchantment', and he added that 'during the whole of this ramble I have had serious thoughts of a cottage. Do not be surprised if my next should inform you that I have taken one'. He added that he had not forgotten that it was proposed that Jack, Stella's brother, should live and farm with them.[56] Would he be satisfied with a cottage and enough land for a cow and some pigs with a garden and 'a philosophical bread & small beer way of living'?[57]

It was no doubt in that 'wild, romantic dell' that the well-known exchange took place:

'Citizen John! this is a fine place to talk treason in!'

'Nay! Citizen Samuel! it is a place to make a man forget that there is any necessity for treason.' [58]

Thelwall was the eldest of the three, and the two younger men respected him for his political role – perhaps were in awe of his notoriety – and acknowledged him as a fellow poet. Many years later Wordsworth recalled him as a man 'of extraordinary talent',[59] while the warmth of Coleridge's feelings was expressed in his letters to him and to others: 'he is intrepid, eloquent and – honest'.[60] Warmed with philosophizing and with eager conversational exchanges, the idea of Thelwall settling among them was taken up seriously. There was even a suggestion that the Thelwalls might move in with William and Dorothy Wordsworth in their over-spacious mansion:[61] could the name of the house, 'All fox den' (Thelwall's spelling), have seemed to be wryly appropriate? Enquiries were made for a cottage. But the poets' generous host and protector, Thomas Poole, the tanner, pulled back from stirring up alarm in the alarmed neighbourhood even further. Were Thelwall to settle there (following upon Coleridge and Wordsworth) 'the whole Malignity of the Aristocrats will converge' upon Poole, and 'riots & dangerous riots might be the consequence'.[62] For many of Poole's neighbours and even relatives shared the view of the spy, Walsh, that he was sheltering a 'mischiefous gang of disaffected Englishmen'.[63]

Thelwall swallowed his disappointment, but the disappointment was grievous. As he left Bridgwater on his way back to Bristol he declared:

> my soul
> Is sick of public turmoil – ah, most sick
> Of the vain effort to redeem a Race
> Enslav'd, because degenerate; lost to Hope,
> Because to Virtue lost – wrapp'd up in Self,

> In sordid avarice, luxurious pomp,
> And profligate intemperance ...

He lamented also the loss of close intercourse with his Samuel:

> Ah 'twould be sweet, beneath the neighb'ring thatch,
> In philosophic amity to dwell,
> Inditing moral verse, or tale, or theme,
> Gay or instructive; and it would be sweet,
> With kindly interchange of mutual aid,
> To delve our little garden plots ...

He cast himself in a tragic role as the innocent victim of persecution:

> ... a Year of miseries,
> Of storms and persecutions, of the pangs
> Of disappointed hope, and keen regrets,
> Wrung from the bosom by a sordid World
> That kindness pays with hatred, and returns
> Evil for good ...[64]

Undoubtedly gossip about this episode got about and inspired the *Anti-Jacobin* to link the names of the poets with Thelwall in the notorious poem of Canning's, 'The New Morality':

> TH-LW-L, and ye that lecture as ye go,
> And for your pains get pelted, praise LEPAUX!

The others invoked in these verses were Coleridge, Southey, Lloyd and Lamb 'and Co' (Wordsworth?), as well as Priestley and Wakefield, and Paine, Helen Maria Williams, Godwin and Holcroft.[65] Thelwall was in eminent company, but he was the only one of these who had played a leading role as a Jacobin activist.

Thelwall returned to Bristol, where he was carefully watched.[66] He spent some days walking through Gloucestershire, where he enjoyed the hospitality of several families:

> some few,
> Still warm and generous, by the changeling world
> Not yet debauch'd, nor to the yoke of fear
> Bending the abject neck: but who, erect
> In conscious principle, still dare to love
> The Man proscrib'd for loving human kind.[67]

Thence Thelwall entered Wales, where no doubt he visited scenes of beauty then being popularized, and where he continued to be watched – perhaps even shadowed. Hazlitt has an anecdote of Thelwall's arrival at an inn in Llangollen. He was sitting at a window awaiting breakfast when a face passed which he could not recognize at the time but which caused him acute unease. Before he realized that it was the face of 'Taylor the spy', a host of impressions and recollections flooded his mind – he recalled his trial for High Treason; he heard 'the speeches of the Attorney and Solicitor-General over again; the gaunt figure of Mr. Pitt glared by him; the walls of a prison enclosed him; and he felt the hands of the executioner near him ...'[68] Taylor was a fervid anti-Jacobin, and if he was indeed shadowing Thelwall it could have been from free-lance zeal.[69] But at last the 'Patriot' seems to have shaken off attentions, and he found a small farm in an isolated village to which he might retire.

II. GONE TO GROUND

Thelwall found himself a refuge at the hamlet of Llys Wen, on the banks of the Wye, seven miles from Hay, nine from Brecknock, eleven from Builth Wells.[70] He wrote in eager anticipation to Thomas Hardy at the end of October 1797 that the farm was about forty acres, 'pretty good land', with a capital orchard; the house 'a handsome & roomy cottage', is 'as desirable a literary retreat as Fancy could have suggested'. His brother-in-law, Jack Vellum, would direct the farming and 'I shall be an apprentice on my own farm'. He and his wife proposed also to take some pupils at thirty guineas a year. He still had to raise the greater part of £270 for stock and crop, etc., and he was inviting friends to contribute: 'as this is a plan for my *permanent* establishment there may perhaps be some persons who would interest themselves about it'.[71] Could Hardy help to 'raise any wind for me by loan or patriotic contribution'? Stella (whom Crabb Robinson described as Thelwall's 'good angel')[72] was setting off from Derby in a few days, with their three children, Maria, Algernon Sidney and Hampden, and with her brother, Jack, and he would shortly follow.[73]

Thelwall's next letter to Hardy is from Hereford (the nearest city in which he could find a library and newspapers), in January 1798. Thelwall was still beset by money problems – the idea of a school had been abandoned – and he was enjoying the simple life:

> We eat as our servants eat – and (as far as the difference of strength produced by different habits will permit) work as they work. I dig – I cart dung and Ashes – I thresh in the barn – I trench the meadows ...In short the political lecturer of Beaufort Buildings is a mere peasant in Llyswen ...

He pictured himself in his rough clothes 'with my spade and my mattock trudging through the village'.[74]

In March he wrote to one of his patrons, Dr Peter
Crompton, declaring that he was 'highly delighted' with his
situation. The health of his family was improving, and he
especially noted the improvement of his eldest child, Maria.
When Maria was an infant, Thelwall had written to Jack
Vellum with an incautious letter in which he assured him that
'the child does not thrive the worse for not being christened
...I hope some time or other [she] will be the happy mother of
a fine hardy race of Republicans & Sans Culottes'.[75] This was
intercepted and passed to a Treasury Solicitor's nark, and held
in the dossier of evidence against Thelwall at his trial for High
Treason! The intellectual 'Jacobins' of the 1790s were
reformers in everything – modes of address,[76] gender and
sexual relations, child nurture, toys and education,[77] styles and
dress. Thelwall reported to Dr Crompton that Maria 'grows a
very stout & vigorous girl':

> We have daily & hourly proofs of the advantages of the stile of
> dress we have adopted, for she bounds along in her trowsers in
> all the romping vivacity of independence, runs up the mount,
> clambers among the rocks, & by her perpetual activity takes
> health by storm.

Thelwall was also delighted with his neighbours, and their
'respectful civility':

> The rustic villagers pay us every mark of attention. Jack & I are
> regarded as a sort of Oracles, our votes are law at all parish
> meetings, we receive & return visits with the farmers & have had
> civil messages from some of the surrounding gentry ...I have
> never in any single instance received the slightest insult since I
> came to settle in Wales; & among the more intelligent part of *the
> people*, the hat is off & the eye brightens whenever I pass by.

However, in one respect this letter marks a change from
his letter to Hardy two months before. He had underestimated

the expenses of commencing farming and was beset with debts. As a result he had given up his share of practical farming and turned to literary pursuits, in the hope of earning a guinea or two from the *Monthly Magazine*, and perhaps more from his projected novel or projected memoirs. In consequence he now had a working day at his desk.[78]

Richard Phillips, the editor of the *Monthly Magazine* was well disposed towards Thelwall, and so was his literary editor, Dr John Aikin. The magazine was successful and could pay well.[79] Thelwall's first contribution may have been on 'The Phenomena of the Wye, during the Winter of 1797-8',[80] a fairly conventional exercise in the picturesque. And this reminds one that Thelwall was not quite as isolated in what he referred to in later life as his 'exile' as might seem. For the Wye was now a celebrated resort for those in search of the beautiful and picturesque. It had been made familiar by William Gilpin's *Observations on the River Wye* (1782), and now was a resort of artists and travellers.[81]

This may be the place to take stock of Thelwall's retirement, in part to redress the embittered account which he himself subsequently gave in the 'Prefatory Memoir'. When Crabb Robinson visited him in October 1799 he found him in 'a very good house & in a beautiful situation'. He had 'a tolerable library' (which he had fetched from London), and 'a very simple unaffected yet sensible woman for his wife, and four young children'.[82] Despite the bad harvest of 1799 Robinson thought that he 'manages better than might be expected of one whose necessities compel him to divide his attention between book making and corn growing'. Apart from his occasional visitors, he maintained a copious correspondence.[83] Some must have been with patrons, like Peter Crompton, and with those who helped to 'raise the wind', like Hardy.[84] But from such fragments of this correspondence as have come to light, and from other

175

inferences, Thelwall was a significant link-figure between circles of advanced reformers and intellectuals in London and the provinces, in such places as Norwich, Derby, Nottingham and Liverpool. In Derby in 1797 he, Stella and the children had been sheltered by Daniels, a silk master, he had been welcomed by some of the 'first people' in the place, and had been invited to conduct a newspaper. He clearly knew many of the 'Roscoe circle' in Liverpool, and, writing to Crompton, he asked to be remembered to 'Raithbone' (another of his patrons),[85] Shepherd,[86] Smith,[87] Rushton,[88] and to Roscoe himself.[89] Dr Peter Crompton had himself recently moved to Liverpool from Derby.[90] There were also one or two eminent bourgeois, like Joseph Strutt of Derby, a son of Jedediah Strutt, (the cotton-spinner and partner to Arkwright), probably another patron of Thelwall's[91] – and perhaps the brothers Wedgwood.[92] If one adds to these names, Thelwall's numerous London acquaintance, and the intellectual circles of George Dyer, William Frend, Coleridge, Wordsworth, Lamb, Southey and Crabb Robinson, as well as the acquaintance he began to gather in Wales and Hereford,[93] he appears as a less solitary figure.

If the label seems helpful it is probably right to see Thelwall in 1797-1802 as an advanced 'bourgeois' reformer[94] who had drifted away from the artisan milieu of the London Corresponding Society. But his connections were not just with isolated pockets of disaffected intellectuals. The extent of disaffection was a good deal wider than that. In the general election of 1802 William Windham, the War Minister and close ally of Pitt (and formerly of Burke), was defeated by a reformer (William Smith) at Norwich. Roscoe was elected in Liverpool in 1806, when he had a very brief and unimpressive parliamentary career. And in Nottingham in 1802 a reformer (Joseph Birch) overturned a sitting member amid extraordinary scenes of triumph. An excited magistrate wrote that in the victory procession were:

> The Goddess of Reason attended by four & twenty Virgins dress'd or rather half dress'd in white in the French fashion followed by the Tree of Liberty and the tri-colour'd Flag; a Band of Music playing the Tune of 'Millions be free' and the multitude singing the chorus.[95]

On appeal to a committee of the House of Commons the election was overthrown.

These examples serve to emphasize that disaffection was widespread until the commencement of the second French War in 1803, and is underestimated in those accounts which present it as declining after the passing of the Two Acts at the end of 1795.[96] But disaffection had no national focus, and this may help to explain why the authorities kept a watch on Thelwall. But the Patriot himself was losing the inclination to play any political role. Perhaps, like Coleridge, he had been deeply dismayed by the French invasion of Switzerland in February 1798.[97] He wrote to Hardy in May that year emphasizing that 'no nation can be free but by its own efforts'. 'As for the French Directory and its faction, nothing appears to me to be further from their design than to leave one atom of liberty either to their own or to any nation.' But he refused any reconciliation with those 'ruffians', Pitt and his ministers:

> But what have we to do with Directories or politics? Peaceful shades of Lyswen! shelter me beneath your luxuriant foliage: lull me to forgetfulness, ye murmuring waters of the Wye. Let me be part farmer and fisherman. But no more politics – no more politics in this bad world![98]

About the same time he wrote to the Welsh scholar and bard, Iolo Morganwg, apologizing for his inability to come and visit him. He had intended to visit the Glamorgan coast, but: 'The state of affairs ...& the prejudices with which I know myself

177

to be watched have made me deem it prudent to lay this intention aside, lest picturesque curiosity, & visits of friendship should be construed into High Treason.[99]

If this was so then it might be construed as treasonable to visit him also. But this did not dissuade Coleridge and William and Dorothy Wordsworth from walking up the Wye, on the spur of the moment, to visit the Thelwalls early in August 1798.[100] William and Dorothy had walked by the Wye only three weeks earlier, as far as Tintern Abbey, where Wordsworth composed his notable 'Lines'.[101] These lines, which have little 'political' reference, recover for us the mood of tranquil affirmation of the 'worshipper of Nature' at this time, although not much is known of the visit to Thelwall, which took place only four or five weeks before the poets took off for Germany. Thelwall (it may be inferred) was not as sanguine as he had been earlier in the year, since he had started to quarrel with his farming neighbours, and he may already have been adopting the posture and self-image of 'the Recluse'. This is perhaps the 'Solitary' whom Wordsworth was later to remember.

We know little as to the reasons for his quarrels with his neighbours. But an example which is striking (in every sense) is that one neighbour clobbered him with a pickaxe in the summer of 1798. This certainly took place. Thelwall took the offender to Brecknock sessions, where he asked for leniency to be shown.[102] Thelwall subsequently implied that this was one of a series of politically motivated persecutions, perhaps encouraged by the local clergyman who whipped up hostilities against him with 'inflammatory allusions from the pulpit'.[103] He also attributed the hostility to 'the animosity which the Welsh are apt enough to entertain ...against every SAXON who intrudes, as a settler, among them'.[104] The second explanation is perhaps nearer to the truth than the first, since Thelwall disclosed elsewhere that the assault arose out of a dispute about a watercourse.[105] This will have been a region of dense, unwritten customs, covering grazing and water rights, which the incomer could easily misunderstand. Thelwall's thirty-six-acre farm was in scattered lots (it took a seven-mile walk to go around it)[106] and he will have had sufficient opportunity to rub against the shins of his farming neighbours: an attempt to divert a customary watercourse could have driven a farmer to fury.

No doubt rumours, inspired by loyalist gentry or clergy, that Thelwall was an undesirable traitor, will have given licence to hostility. But there were other reasons; Thelwall's 'fits of abstraction, his solitary rambles, among the woods and dingles' gave him the reputation among the more credulous of being a conjuror who walked in the woods 'to talk with his evil spirits'.[107] During the hue and cry after a felon his house was besieged. The less credulous may have been irritated by his curiosity, by the critical eye which he cast over their work. With his customary over-confidence Thelwall was already writing in the *Monthly Magazine* only a year after he moved in, as an authority on agriculture in South Wales.[108] His neighbours may not all have been readers of the magazine, but they were able to identify a know-all. Thelwall's full list of complaints against the customs of the country did not appear until eighteen months later, and it was expressed with a vehemence which is almost comic.

Thelwall lamented 'the pestiferous ignorance and indolence' of the farmers. 'All their delight is in their horses, which however in general are but a sorry set of mongrels.' They used too many horses at plough. They did not know how to cultivate winter feed, such as turnips:

> Cow-cabbages we grow none. And indeed neither the morality of the people nor of their stock admit of such expensive cultivation. Of the former, there are several in this very neighbourhood, who carry on every species of petty

179

depredation ...who follow their calling as a regular and reputable trade, and thrive in the world ...by robbing gardens, orchards, and hen-roosts. Nay some there are who have even by such and the like reputable practices, become landed gentlemen of Wales ...What chance would a field of winter cabbages have in such a neighbourhood ...

But should your neighbours spare your cabbages, be assured their stock would not. There are certain maxims of Welsh morality ...which, though hitherto only traditionarily and practically handed down (like the common law of England heretofore) it may be useful and instructive to reduce ...into writing – to wit – It is lawful and right to keep twenty times as much stock (particularly sheep) as you have land to maintain; to consider all the farms in the neighbourhood as a common; to graze everything your neighbour has upon his ground, ripe or unripe, except his wheat; and abuse him if he murmurs or complains. It is lawful and right to turn your horses, when idle, loose upon the roads, to shift for themselves, tear down your neighbour's hedges, and destroy his hay or grain. It is lawful and right to keep pigs which you never feed, and turn them loose without yoke or ring, so that no hedge or fence may be able to resist them ...All this is perfectly right and moral – but to pound your neighbour's horse, or sheep, or pig ...or even to set your dog to worry and tear the ears of an intruder ...these are enormities with which rape or highway-robbery and murder are scarcely to be put in competition ...[109]

This 'morality' was supported not only by the predators themselves but also by 'a good sort of friendly people' who tolerated such 'established usages'. But the worst reference of all was reserved for the sheep:

The morals of the very sheep are contaminated, and their manners corrupted by the circumstances under which they live. In the midst of cultivation, and with the marks of proprietorship on their backs and ears, they have all the habits of savage nature. With the wildness and nimbleness of untamed dogs ...they leap your garden walls and your hedges, as the wolves of old were used to leap their pin-folds. I planted a thousand cow-cabbages in my garden last year; ...but behold, my neighbour's sheep scaled the wall during a hard frost, and devoured and spoiled about four fifths of them ...[110]

Such delinquent sheep are not unknown in the mountainous parts of Wales to this day. They need not have been politically motivated.

Thelwall was an outsider from the network of relationships and the exchanges of services which supported the Brecon small farmers, and no doubt predators thought him fair game. He turned increasingly to his literary pursuits, spending several months on a Saxon epic, 'The Hope of Albion'. But this work was interrupted by the public descent of a King's Messenger upon a wagon from London at Hay-on-Wye, where a parcel of books addressed to Thelwall, as well as letters, were seized. 'All the furious passions of an alarmed and ignorant neighbourhood were set once more afloat ...the Recluse and his family were again exposed to all the bitterness of vulgar insult ...'[111] After this, neither the incoming nor the outgoing posts were secure. Disheartened, he abandoned 'The Hope of Albion'. This was perhaps no great loss to literature, although the passages which he published, by way of an advertisement, in *Poems Chiefly Written in Retirement* are somewhat more promising than the mediocre contents of the rest of that book.[112] In truth, Thelwall evinced more ambition than achievement as a poet, and Coleridge wrote with justice that he was 'deficient in that patience of mind which can look intensely and frequently at the same subject. He believes and disbelieves with impassioned confidence'.[113]

At some time in the first half of 1799 it seems that Stella's brother, Jack, left them, and Thelwall had to resume his part in the farming. By September it was clear that the

1799 harvest would be a disaster. He wrote to Hardy that he was 'almost harassed & tormented to death by the perversness of the season'. Torrents of rain were deluging the fields and destroying the crops. He was going to suffer a serious loss.[114] But another loss which he suffered at the end of the year was more terrible and more unexpected. The *Monthly Magazine* carried in its columns of deaths:

> At Llys-Wen, Brecknockshire, aged 6 years, (of the croup), Frances Maria Thelwall, a child whose premature expansion of mind, whose endearing manners and benevolent disposition had rendered her an object of affection in all the various circles of society in which (young as she was) the peculiar fortunes of her parents had occasioned her to be known.[115]

This was the girl whom we last encountered bounding the hills in her trousers. Her parents were quite broken up, and for months John Thelwall was writing pathetic poetical effusions for Maria:

> whose sweet smiles
> And fair expanding beauties, thro' the night
> Of my disastrous destiny diffus'd
> A soothing radiance ...[116]

By the summer Stella's health also gave cause for alarm, and she went to Hereford to stay with friends.

Thelwall was utterly sorry for himself, and not afraid to show it. He had posed as the Patriot and then as the Recluse and failed in both roles. Every bit of the fault fell upon others – his persecutors, the predators – and he pictured himself as:

> O'erwhelm'd with cares and sorrows! while thou striv'd'st
> With thy hard Destiny, with carking toil,
> Solicitous, to snatch thy scanty means
> From prowling Plunder, or the inclement rage
> Of an ungenial season ...[117]

He was not so much aware (in 1800) of political persecution:

> ... now no more, with her insensate howl,
> The demon Persecution, tir'd intrudes
> On my sequester'd privacy ...[118]

But that he was still a target for surveillance was disclosed when he visited Merthyr, in June and perhaps also in September shortly before the great riots (for which he was blamed).[119] In fact his mind was on other things. He had commenced a novel, *The Daughter of Adoption*, and had walked up to London with a chapter in his pocket, where he succeeded in selling it to Phillips of St Paul's Church Yard, and gaining an advance. He completed one-third, and the work was then long delayed, then 'upwards of two thirds ...was hurried through in the course of a few weeks, amidst all the bustle of the *deceitful harvest*' of 1800. The novel reads like that. The first volume contains some passages of social criticism, but the final three volumes are mere conventional money-spinners.[120] Towards the end of the year the landlord pushed him out of his tenancy amidst much acrimony. It had been a disillusioning experience:

> From 'Theatres and Halls of Assembly' to a little Village of only twenty miserable cottages – from the friendly, the enlightened, the animated circles of Norwich – from the elegant and highly intellectual society of Derby, to the sordid ignorance of a neighbourhood whose boorish inhabitants hash up a barbarous jargon of corrupted Welsh, with still more corrupted English ...was another of those sudden transitions by which the faculties are necessarily stunned and stupified.[121]

The Recluse therefore joined Stella in Hereford, a 'neighbourhood, whose superior civilization ...secures his safety, and protects him from insult'.[122] There he busied himself with literary pursuits and with researches into Nordic,

183

Saxon and Celtic antiquities, presumably for his 'Hope of Albion'.[123] Next year he told his patron, Joseph Strutt of Derby, that he had undergone a 'metamorphose':

> Nothing of the plain out-of-fashioned singularity of the old republican remains, but in my heart – and there it is smothered in silence, except when with a chosen few I can indulge my native energies. In dress, in manners, etc I assimilate myself with all possible diligence to the fashion of the times, assume the pride and port of a man of some importance, and aspire to the reputation of every aristocractical accomplishment. In short, a persecution would not suffer me to crawl upon the earth, I am trying what can be done by soaring into the clouds.[124]

He had confidently assumed a new career, as a lecturer and teacher in elocution.[125] Nothing survived of the Patriot except his fading notoriety.

III. THE KILL

It was left to Wordsworth and Coleridge to make the kill. Although Thelwall had been silenced politically, he had not confessed his errors – nor did he do so; indeed, in the post-war years he attempted a political re-entry. He had lost, in his Llys-Wen years, his buoyancy and 'impassioned confidence'; the death of Maria seemed to leave him as less. Even so, the 'Jacobinism' with which he was peculiarly associated had not been altogether discredited.

As the decade drew to a close, loyalists caricatured every form of liberal or innovative opinion as 'Jacobinism'. In this they followed Burke, who had declared that one-fifth of the political nation, or some eighty thousand people, were 'pure Jacobins; utterly incapable of amendment; objects of eternal vigilance'. Thelwall disdained to give in to the assault and to disavow his sympathy for Jacobin principles. He wrote in the *Rights of Nature*:

> I adopt the term *Jacobinism* without hesitation -
>
> 1.Because it is fixed upon us, as a stigma, by our enemies ...
>
> 2.Because, though I abhor the sanguinary ferocity of the late Jacobins in France, yet their principles ...are the most consonant with my ideas of reason, and the nature of man, of any that I have met with ...I use the term Jacobinism simply to indicate *a large and comprehensive system of reform, not professing to be built upon the authorities and principles of the Gothic custumary.*[126]

The loyalist use of 'Jacobin' he was, subsequently, to describe as a 'popular cant nick name ...a term of no definable signification, but conjuring up in the minds of alarmist & zealous royalists every emotion that belongs to the hatred of all crimes & enormities'.[127] Much the same view had been expressed by Charles Lamb: '*all* persons and *all* things, to which these calumniators are *hostile* ...are *Jacobins* and *Jacobinical*'. They 'pass sentence of *Jacobinism backwards* upon such men as Milton, Sidney, Harrington and Locke'.[128]

But who were in fact the avowed Jacobins? They were few: Tom Paine was exiled; and the corresponding societies had few nationally known leaders. The *Anti-Jacobin* concentrated its fire upon Foxite peers and politicians and liberal newspapers. But for a popularly known target John Thelwall would serve. In Gillray's famous print of 'The New Morality' – a pull-out in the *Anti-Jacobin Review* (July 1798) – he is seated on the very head of the beast (Bedford), and ahead of Fox. He continues to be a stock figure of polemic, both in caricature and in writing. He featured as 'Citizen Rant' in George Walker's *The Vagabond* (1799), and as 'Citizen Rant' in Isaac D'Israeli's *Vaurien*. The portrait in the latter was so transparent and malicious that the Analytical Review feared that it might incite readers to attack the subject: 'it may be attended with infinite danger to the individual'.[129]

As Coleridge and Wordsworth grew more conservative and conformist in their views it is no wonder that they wished to distance themselves from so notorious a figure. There was no sudden rupture between Thelwall and either poet. Coleridge maintained a correspondence for several years, expressing no agreement on matters political or religious but 'plain simple affection'.[130] But when he was unwell in April 1801 Coleridge wrote in terms which must have dismayed Thelwall:

> we are so utterly unlike each other in our habits of thinking, and we have adopted such irreconcileably different opinions in Politics, Religion, & Metaphysics, (& probably in Taste too) that ...such, I fear, is the chasm between us, that so far from being able to shake hands across it, we cannot even make our Words intelligible to each other.

He continued to express 'Moral Esteem, frequent & kind wishes, & a lively Interest in your Welfare as a good Man & man of Talents'. That was that, except that Coleridge added, in a seeming afterthought, 'I am sure I need not request you not to mention my name in your memoirs'.[131]

Not to be discouraged, Thelwall ventured to call on the poets in late November 1803 as he made his way to Scotland to deliver lectures on elocution. He dined with Mrs Wordsworth and Dorothy at Grasmere, and Wordsworth himself arrived from Keswick just as he was leaving. Thelwall went on to Keswick, to visit Southey and Coleridge, and also Hazlitt (who was staying there). His comments on the company are not altogether complimentary. As to Coleridge he had nothing to say (when writing to Stella). Sara Coleridge 'seems only improved by becoming less talkative (i.e. less obvious)'. Mrs Southey's 'only expression is vanity, & she seems a mere mute in the drama':

> Even S.[outhey] himself towers above his fellow beings more by his vanity than his genius. He *looks* like a man who has read more than he has thought, & who has fancy without energy & *when* he speaks, you perceive, even in the very tuning of his most *execrable* voice which is half way between a croak & a screach, rather the formality of the reader than the ease of the conversationalist.

Thelwall was more pleased with 'the disputatious metaphysical Hazlet *[sic.]*'. He is 'a very improved young man. His mind has unfolded. He has become less disputatious & more conversable'. Hazlitt accompanied him on his way to Penrith, and they exclaimed at the beauties of the landscape together.[132]

The company at Keswick perhaps avoided sensitive political issues, although Thelwall later recollected that Southey 'expressly stated, & C[oleridge] tacitly admitted that the second [war] was only the *rump*, or necessary consequence of the first'.[133] Coleridge also held forth in his paradoxical way on religious questions.[134] This was perhaps the last occasion on which Thelwall met Wordsworth and Coleridge, although some contact was kept with Southey. The distance had been struck, without acrimony, and in later life all three poets referred to Thelwall with patronizing goodwill. And Thelwall also, it seems, cherished warm memories of their intercourse, if we are to credit the account of his widow, Cecil,[135] for when she was preparing her memoir of her husband she wrote to Wordsworth recalling that 'Thelwall often spoke of the friendly intercourse, which at one time subsisted between you, with much pleasure: and always spoke of you with much admiration and friendship'. But she had been well schooled, and hastened to add that 'I do not wish to have any political reference to the acquaintance which then subsisted between you ...'.[136]

Thelwall went on from Keswick to deliver his lectures on elocution in Scotland. He was attempting, with mixed success, to change his identity. He was a very successful practical elocutionist, having cured himself of a slight lisp in youth, and his later prowess as an orator was undeniable.[137] He was now developing elocution as a science, and developing cures for speech defects, and scholars regard his work with some respect.[138] He was delighted with his success, and (he wrote to Hardy) he was confident that this new career would provide for 'the comfortable establishment' of his family.[139] 'You are for peace, you say', he wrote again to Hardy; 'Very well – Peace be with you, both here & hereafter. I am for Elocution!!! Cicero & Demosthenes for ever! Huzza!!!!!'.[140] But his triumph did not extend to Edinburgh, where he delivered upon himself a self-inflicted wound.

The recently launched *Edinburgh Review* had already indicated its dislike of the poets of *Lyrical Ballads*, and also its particular hostility to Thelwall. In April 1803 it published a contemptuous review of Thelwall's *Poems Chiefly Written in Retirement*: the review was anonymous but was known to be by the magazine's editor, Francis Jeffrey. It sneered at Thelwall's low social origins, and suggested that he had been better advised to remain on a tailor's bench, 'to cut out cashmere, or stitch in buckram', than to attempt a political or literary career. The review was mainly a sarcastic recital of the 'Prefatory Memoir' in the volume; in short, it was a snobbish send-up.[141] The hostility was taken further. When Thelwall's course of lectures commenced on 8 December 1803, it came to an abrupt end on the first night, owing to barracking and laughter which (Thelwall believed) was orchestrated by Jeffrey himself from behind a screen.[142] Thelwall was injured to the quick, in his self-esteem (a large organ), in his literary reputation, and in his very livelihood. He hurriedly wrote a pamphlet attacking Jeffrey: it is poor stuff, with no wit and much self-justification. He argued that:

> During the last seven years of my life, it is true, I have abjured all politics: – from my soul I have abjured them. I am wedded – enthusiastically wedded, to a very different pursuit. But have I *shifted sides*, like a common prize fighter? Have I withdrawn myself from one party, only to display my violence for another? ...As a politician, I am absolutely *defunct*: but I have not started forth, in regenerated wickedness, a slanderer, or persecutor; nor do I quit my Church Yard, in the ghastly shroud of Criticism, to cross the way of any human being; – to haunt him with the remembrances of things that are past ...

No: but Thelwall could scarcely complain of Jeffrey alluding to his political past, for his own 'Prefatory Memoir' dwelt on this.

Jeffrey came back with a spirited (and more witty) reply:

> It is rather mortifying ...to the pride of philosophy to observe

how little Mr Thelwall seems to have profited from his long experience of persecution and abuse. After having had his chair and desk overturned by the peace-officers in the Borough ...after being nearly murdered at Yarmouth, Lynn, Wisbeach, Norwich, Stockport, and Derby (at the first of which places he was nearly carried off to Kamtschatka), ...after being 'successively attacked by the Sailors, the Armed Associators, and the Inniskilling Dragoons' ...and 'ferociously assaulted with a pick-axe' by a rustic royalist at Llyswen – it is really wonderful that he should take it so violently amiss, that a few nameless critics should laugh at his Book, and some idle young men at his Lectures.[144]

And to this Thelwall replied in a pamphlet as bad-tempered and as unwitty as the first.[145]

Thelwall sent his first pamphlet to Wordsworth, and a letter (which has not survived) perhaps eliciting his support. Wordsworth sent back a long and characteristically egotistical reply, in which he complained of the *Review*'s treatment, not of Thelwall but of himself – a letter which managed to express goodwill while avoiding any attention to the issues.[146] Thelwall retreated to Glasgow, but in his usual state of self-deluding over-confidence. He was convinced that he was the victor in the exchange, and (according to Coleridge) he wrote to Dr Crompton a letter:

> which for honest-hearted drunken self-gloting Vanity in the delirium of Triumph surely never had it's like ['I have left Edinburgh dismayed & contrite; Glasgow, it is believed, will rush forward eagerly to wipe off the stain, which, she deems, Edinburgh has brought on Scotland['] &c &c &c – & far worse.[147]

No blame can attach to the poets for not coming to the aid of such delusion. For Thelwall was not the victor of the exchange. The 'stain', if there was any, remained his.

The political fox was now dead. And there matters may

be left until the end of the French Wars, with the publication in 1817 of Coleridge's *Biographia Literaria* and in 1814 of Wordsworth's *Excursion*. Neither makes any explicit reference to Thelwall, but both are concerned with exorcizing the Jacobin ghost in the poets' past. Coleridge had already attempted this in the *Friend*: 'I may safely defy my worst enemy to shew, in any of my few writings, the least bias to Irreligion, Immorality, or Jacobinism ...'[148] To which Robert Southey expostulated, 'if he was not a Jacobine, in the common acceptance of the name, I wonder who the Devil was'.[149] In *Biographia Literaria* he confected a more extensive, either dishonest or self-deluding, gloss upon his past, and by good fortune Thelwall's annotated copy survives. Where Coleridge declared, of his *Watchman* years, 'how opposite even then my principles were to those of Jacobinism or even of democracy', Thelwall noted: 'Mr C. was indeed far from Democracy, because he was far beyond it, I well remember – for he was a down right zealous leveller & indeed in one of the worst senses of the word he was a Jacobin, a man of blood ...' And where Coleridge wrote 'I retired to a cottage at Stowey', Thelwall interpolated:

> Where I visitted him & found him a decided Leveller – abusing the democrats for their hypocritical moderatism, in pretending to be willing to give people equallity of privileges & rank, while, at the same time, they would refuse them all that the others could be valuable for – equality of property – or rather abolition of all property.

And when Coleridge comes to describe modern German drama as 'jacobinical', Thelwall had a more extended comment. The term 'Jacobin':

> is used by the consistent Mr C. in such a way as to be apparently applicable to all reformers & *incliners* to republicanism – in short to all who are dissatisfied with the

established systems of *legitimate* despotism: & then everything
that is immoral & detestable in arts literature manners & habits
…is to be called Jacobinical also; & the logical conclusion is
expected to follow that everything immoral & detestable is
concentrated & personified in the said reformers &c. – He does
not call those from whom *he has deserted* 'spawn of Hell' – He
only endeavours to lead the minds of his readers to think (or at
least to feel) of them as such.[150]

Several of Coleridge's subsequent writings were to confirm
this diagnosis.

I do not recall any occasion in these years when
Wordsworth disavowed his own 'Jacobin' past so publicly and
explicitly. He did this by proxy and the proxy was the figure of
the Solitary in the *Excursion*. Marilyn Butler has helpfully
presented the *Excursion* as the central text in the 'War of the
Intellectuals' in the post-war years.[151] The poem is a
'commemoration of victory', of England over the French
Revolution, and of Christian orthodoxy over Jacobinism: it is
(in Marilyn Butler's words) 'a poem which aspires to
permanence in a traditional institutional, orthodox Christian
vein'. Her judgement does not differ greatly from that of
Francis Jeffrey at the time: the doctrine that the work is
intended to enforce is that 'a firm belief in the providence of a
wise and beneficent Being must be our great stay and support
under all afflictions and perplexities upon earth – and that
there are indications of his power and goodness in all the
aspects of the visible universe …'[152] Hence the poem, which
is at times heavily didactic, seeks to inculcate the greatest
deference not only towards the Supreme Being but also
towards Nature.

There are, of course, passages where what Hazlitt called
Wordsworth's 'levelling Muse' can be seen at work; Jeffrey
was irritated at finding philosophy presented through the
mouth of a Pedlar (the Wanderer), 'a person accustomed to

higgle about tape, or brass sleeve buttons ...A man who went about selling flannel and pocket-handkerchiefs in this lofty diction, would soon frighten away all his customers'.[153] He was also critical of the attention given to dalesmen and to humble cottagers. But to those reformers who remained among Wordsworth's admirers this democratic impulse was slight compensation for the manifest submission of the poet to established authority, spiritual and temporal. For the sympathy with lowly subjects was never permitted to lead on to democratic conclusions, whether political or doctrinal. And the *Excursion* remained, for generations of Wordsworth's contemporaries, his major exercise in philosophical poetry, for the *Prelude* was not published until 1850.

It is the part of the Solitary in the *Excursion*'s plot to negate any aspirations to political reform. His story is twice recounted, once in Book II by the Wanderer, again in Book III by himself. The chaplain to a Highland regiment, he formed a happy marriage with two lovely children, and (promptly to Wordsworth's habitual mournful machinery) mother and children both died. The disconsolate widower found consolation in 'the voice of social transport' heard from revolutionary France. He shared in:

> A proud and most presumptuous confidence
> In the transcendent wisdom of the age,
> And her discernment; not alone in rights,
> And in the origin and bounds of power
> Social and temporal; but in laws divine,
> Deduced by reason, or to faith revealed.
> An overweening trust was raised; and fear
> Cast out, alike of person and of thing.
> Plague from this union spread, whose subtle bane
> The strongest did not easily escape;
> And He, what wonder! took a mortal taint.
> How shall I trace the change, how bear to tell

That he broke faith with them whom he had laid
In earth's dark chambers, with a Christian's hope!
An infidel contempt of holy writ
Stole by degrees upon his mind; and hence
Life, like that Roman Janus, double-faced;
Vilest hypocrisy – the laughing, gay
Hypocrisy, not leagued with fear, but pride.
Smooth words he had to wheedle simple souls;
But, for disciples of the inner school,
Old freedom was old servitude, and they
The wisest whose opinions stooped the least
To known restraints; and who most boldly drew
Hopeful prognostications from a creed,
That, in the light of false philosophy,
Spread like a halo round a misty moon,
Widening its circle as the storms advance.[154]

At length he renounced 'his sacred function' and enjoyed
'the unshackled layman's natural liberty':

Speech, manners, morals, all without disguise.
I do not wish to wrong him; though the course
Of private life licentiously displayed
Unhallowed actions – planted like a crown
Upon the insolent aspiring brow
Of spurious notions – worn as open signs
Of prejudice subdued ...[155]

In Book III much the same tale is rehearsed by the Solitary
himself, with further suggestions of 'unhallowed actions' as the
zealots disbanded, quarrelled among themselves, or turned to
more extreme courses:

Among men
So charactered did I maintain a strife
Hopeless, and still more hopeless every hour;
But, in the process, I began to feel
That, if the emancipation of the world

Were missed, I should at least secure my own,
And be in part compensated. For rights
Widely – inveterately usurped upon,
I spake with vehemence; and promptly seized
All that Abstraction furnished for my needs
Or purposes; nor scrupled to proclaim,
And propagate, by liberty of life,
Those new persuasions.[156]

Many years later, in 1843, Wordsworth dictated to Isabella Fenwick a note in which he professed that the Solitary was modelled upon several persons 'who fell under my observation during frequent residences in London at the beginning of the French Revolution':

> The chief of these was, one may *now* say, a Mr. Fawcett, a preacher at a dissenting meeting-house at the Old Jewry ...But ...like many others in those times of like shewy talents, he had not strength of character to withstand the effects of the French Revolution, and of the wild and lax opinions which had done so much towards producing it, and far more in carrying it forward in its extremes. Poor Fawcett, I have been told, became pretty much such a person as I have described; and early disappeared from the stage, having fallen into habits of intemperance, which I have heard (though I will not answer for the fact) hastened his death ...there were many like him at that time, which the world will never be without ...[157]

Of course in any creative work a character may be composed of several models and inventions; but one suspects that this note was intended to throw readers off the scent. Fawcett has been carefully investigated and he fits the Solitary's part very ill. He contributed perhaps only the element of the charismatic preacher. 'A patient search', George McLean Harper remarked, 'has failed to discover anything derogatory to his character, and the gossip about him which Wordsworth heard is only an instance of the way in which men's reputations were assailed by those who took for granted that heterodox opinions must of necessity spring from a wicked heart and end in an evil life'.[158] But Hazlitt, who testified warmly to his admiration for Fawcett ('Of all the persons I have ever known, he was the most perfectly free from every taint of jealousy or narrowness'), added that: 'He was one of the most enthusiastic admirers of the French Revolution; and I believe the disappointment of the hopes he had cherished of the freedom and happiness of mankind, preyed upon his mind and hastened his death'.[159] He may indeed have 'fallen into habits of intemperance', as Wordsworth said, but this was not a habit attributed to the Solitary.

But there is of course in Thelwall a model for the Solitary very much closer to Wordsworth's life and inner conflicts. Indeed, Thelwall might have posed for his own self-portrait as the Solitary. Looking back, he referred to his 'spleenful solitude at Llyswen'. He at times called himself – as Wordsworth calls the Solitary – 'the Recluse'. He described his state of mind as 'a mournful picture of the soreness and irritability of a mind equally out of humour with itself and all the world'.[160] It is difficult to read the approach to the Solitary in Book II and *not* to bring Thelwall to mind:[161]

> The glory of the times fading away -
> The splendor, which had given a festal air
> To self-importance, hallowed it, and veiled
> From his own sight – this gone, he forfeited
> All joy in human nature; was consumed,
> And vexed, and chafed, by levity and scorn,
> And fruitless indignation; galled by pride;
> Made desperate by contempt of men who throve
> Before his sight in power or fame, and won,
> Without desert, what he desired; weak men,
> Too weak even for his envy or his hate!
> Tormented thus, after a wandering course
> Of discontent, and inwardly opprest

With malady – in part, I fear, provoked
By weariness of life – he fixed his home,
Or, rather say, sate down by very chance,
Among these rugged hills; where now he dwells,
And wastes the sad remainder of his hours,
Steeped in self-indulging spleen, that wants not
Its own voluptuousness; – on this resolved,
With this content, that he will live and die
Forgotten, – at safe distance from 'a world
Not moving to his mind.'

Cumberland supplies most of the topography for the *Excursion*, but the Brecon Beacons, west of Llys Wen, supply plenty of 'rugged hills'. There are even hints that Wordsworth recalled more literal details of his visit there in 1798. Earlier in that year Thelwall had written to Dr Crompton, describing:

> Across one end of our orchard flows a pretty little brook ...thro a small romantic dingle to empty itself into the Wye. In which with hobbyhorsical industry I have built a cascade of 8 or 9 feet height & am making a rude hermitage (a sequestered summer study) in the dingle beneath. The boy [his son Sidney] has found out this place & is as delighted with it as myself ...

The boy would spend whole hours listening to the water – 'the old women say he will be drowned, I say he will be philosophised'. And he added, in Wordsworthian vein, 'His violent passions will acquire, as he grows up, the curb of meditativeness. I know, by experience, the power & influence of such habits; & my maxim is, that Seneca and Socrates preach well, but rocks & brooks & waterfalls much better'.[162]

Beside this description of his 'hobbyhorse (my cascade & hermitage)' one might set several passages of the *Excursion*. Thus in Book II the Pedlar and the Poet come upon 'a penthouse' erected among rocks, with the help of a child's hands, where – horrors! – they found a copy of *Candide*, 'dull product of a scoffer's pen'.[163] Even more striking are several passages in Book III descriptive of a 'hidden nook' beneath rocks down which water descended, a nook which the Solitary described as his 'Druid cromlech', and in the vicinity of which a 'fair-faced cottage boy' is busy 'mending the defects / Left in the fabric of a leaky dam'.[164] The characters linger for a long while in this nook:

> That seemed for self-examination made;
> Or, for confession, in the sinner's need,
> Hidden from all men's view.[165]

Undoubtedly Thelwall will have led Wordsworth and Coleridge to his hobby-horse, and traces of the memory survived.

But the identification of Thelwall as the primary, most significant and most acutely felt model for the Solitary does not rest upon these small indications. It lies far more in the inwardness of the theme, in the self-examination of a scoffing, rationalist, but enthusiastic and responsive mind. One may hope that this essay has sufficiently revealed this, and it should perhaps be added that Thelwall on several occasions declared that he was not a Christian;[166] whether he was a convinced atheist, or a 'theist', is less clear.[167] Of course, Wordsworth will have mixed, in the Godwin circle, with many other rationalists and sceptics, some of them, like Basil Montagu, more close to him than Thelwall. No over-literal identification can be proposed. In one sense the Solitary is a composite portrait, to which Thelwall, Fawcett, and others may have contributed. In another, and important, sense, the model for the Solitary was Wordsworth himself – or Wordsworth's Jacobin alter ego. This had been seen at once by Hazlitt: 'His thoughts are his real subject ...He sees all things in himself ...Even the dialogues ...are soliloquies of the same character, taking different views of the subject. The recluse, the pastor, and the pedlar, are three persons in one poet'.[168]

This was partly due to Wordsworth's 'intense intellectual egotism'. Hazlitt said, 'The power of his mind preys upon itself. It is as if there were nothing but himself and the universe'.[169] But we have to go on to say that in the transition from the great version of the *Prelude* in 1805 to the *Excursion* nine years later we are witnessing a sad decline in poetic energies and authenticity. Critics have long noticed this, although very few at the time knew enough about the unpublished *Prelude* to mark the contrast. Apart from those passages of the *Excursion* composed in the earlier years – notably Book I, 'The Ruined Cottage'[170] – the sense of philosophy as lived experience gives way to dutiful didacticism. In the *Prelude* we are placed directly in the presence of belief: in the *Excursion* we are told what we ought to believe. The 1805 *Prelude* is indeed a heroic essay in self-revelation. From 1795 to 1805 – for fully ten years – Wordsworth laboured both to recover honestly and to compose into art the Jacobin experience and its disappointment. The poem was composed while he was still in a state of conflict. But at some point after 1805[171] he conceived of the figure of the Solitary, and the Jacobin experience (which had also been part of himself) was simply extruded, set out there, as an outside object, the Solitary, a target for criticism and censure. That part of the poet's self thus extruded is no longer acknowledged as any part of his own sensibility. And even the opportunity for the dramatization of conflict is not taken: Poet, Pedlar and Parson go on and on at the Solitary, instructing him in good and proper views, and the object of this instruction is given few good lines in which to reply.

This is far from the method of the *Prelude*. We are drawn within the vortex of the conflict. While Wordsworth faces the failure of utopian expectations, he affirms and conveys the force of utopianism. He does not extrude it as an object for

199

external censure. Of the Terror:

> Most melancholy at that time, O Friend!
> Were my day-thoughts, my dreams were miserable;
> Through months, through years, long after the last beat
> Of those atrocities (I speak bare truth,
> As if to thee alone in private talk)
> I scarcely had one night of quiet sleep
> Such ghastly visions had I of despair
> And tyranny, and implements of death,
> And long orations which in dreams I pleaded
> Before unjust Tribunals, with a voice
> Labouring, a brain confounded, and a sense,
> Of treachery and desertion in the place
> The holiest that I knew of, my own soul.[172]

It is an extraordinary image, because he is pleading before the unjust tribunal of his own soul. There is no passage comparable to this in the *Excursion*. The finger of guilt may be pointed at the Solitary, but there is no sense that his interlocutors share any responsibility for the historical process. That lies somewhere outside their complacent souls. And in any revolutionary process the worst are destined to win:

> For by superior energies; more strict
> Affiance in each other; faith more firm
> In their unhallowed principles, the bad
> Have fairly earned a victory o'er the weak,
> The vacillating, inconsistent good.[173]

This is Burke put into verse.[174]

The Solitary is a way in which Wordsworth could put a part of himself outside himself, a self-disowning. But what is disowned is not only himself, it is also the possibility of rational affirmative political action – to remake institutions and laws, to challenge custom and Gothic forms. The very pretence of such aspiration is now presented as an object of scorn. So that, in turning back to the domestic affections and relations, Wordsworth is in some sense evicting the public virtues from history.

The Solitary, then, is the failure of Wordsworth's own Jacobinical *alter ego* objectified and manipulated. 'I do not mean to wrong him' – yet wrong him he did. And if we see John Thelwall as a model, then the manipulation is more clear. For Thelwall was driven into despondent solitude not only by his own weaknesses and disappointed illusions and 'the failure of the French Revolution' but by the bearing down of the whole of established culture and established power upon him. The absent evidence in the *Excursion* is that of the counter-revolution. Yet his picture of 'Jacobinism' was profoundly influential in the nineteenth century, and has even seen a recent revival in the bicentennial obituaries on the French Revolution.

We should conclude by signalling what was the actual political resting-place of the model for the Solitary. Like many reformers Thelwall supported the second war against France. He even wrote a *Poem and Oration on the Death of Lord Nelson* (1805), while he mended his fences with the Foxite Whigs with a *Monody* on the death of Charles James Fox (1806). At the end of 1805 he wrote a long letter to Thomas Hardy in which he rehearsed his political views:

> Whoever may be regarded as the guilty cause of the present war (which I confess I regard as the rump & connected consequence of the last ...) I do not regard it as a question between one form or one principle of government and another – but as a struggle to decide whether ambitious France shall grasp the universal sovreignty of Europe, & Britain be a depopulated province? – A question which I am confident in my own mind, must ultimately be decided upon our own shores ...I confess to you, that (with all the smarting remembrance of my wrongs about me) I am ready to use my present chains as

weapons against the foe, rather than submit to the heavier fetters which *Imperial* France would impose.

Even when France was Republican; & Republican speculations were carried to the greatest extent among us, you know very well, that I was never one of those who would have looked to a French army for English liberty, or have been found among the ranks of the Invader: but from the moment when Buonaparte set foot on the territory of Egypt, I no longer considered the struggle between the two countries as a question of principles but of power ...

Such were my speculations even in my spleenful solitude at Llyswen. Still, however, my admiration waited upon the personal qualities of Buonaparte – still I endeavoured to believe that he was something more than a mere ambitious soldier – that he was not merely the greatest of mankind – that he would show the world that it was possible to be at once great and good; to have great military talents, & yet to reverence Liberty. When afterwards, the Republican Mussulman became a Catholic Consul, I did not instantaneously give him up (as some of the best friends of Liberty in this nation did) nor did I hold to him with the enthusiastic confidence which seemed, as I thought, to infatuate you & some others. I kept my mind upon the balance & watched his motions – judging him by his own Acts & his own state proclamations. These, however, did not leave me long in doubt. Step by step, with the most profound and specious policy, I saw him advancing to the usurpation of all power, & the destruction of every sacred principle of Freedom ...

It was the 'tyrant Buonaparte, who has destroyed, perhaps for ever, all my glorious speculations of the improvability of man, & blasted the best hopes of Europe'.[175]
Some of those lines might have been spoken by the Solitary. Thelwall did not join that slender band, which included Hazlitt, who took refuge in a truculent Bonapartism.

E.P. THOMPSON

It is not known whether he recognized his own portrait in the Solitary. He spoke highly of the *Excursion*, although complaining that Wordsworth borrowed from himself without acknowledgement – but it is not clear in what the 'borrowing' consisted.[176] He stands as yet one more example of the hazards which descend upon reformers who allow their political hopes or strategies to become too much involved with the outcome of developments in other countries. We have seen sufficient examples of this in our own time.

NOTES

1. John Thelwall in the *Champion*, 6 June 1819.
2. See *John Thelwall: Political Writings*, ed. Gregory Claeys (forthcoming); Iain Hampsher-Monk, 'John Thelwall and the Eighteenth-Century Radical Response to Political Economy', *Hist. Jl*, xxxiv (1991); Geoffrey Gallop, 'Ideology and the English Jacobins: The Case of John Thelwall', *Enlightenment and Dissent*, v (1986).
3. See Thomas Holcroft, *A Letter to the Right Honourable William Windham* (London, 1795).
4. Thelwall withdrew for a while from the L.C.S. but resumed a place in its leadership in the campaign against the passing of the Two Acts at the end of 1795: Albert Goodwin, *The Friends of Liberty* (London, 1979), pp. 364, 389. John Horne Tooke stood unsuccessfully as parliamentary candidate for Westminster in 1796.
5. [Cecil Thelwall], *The Life of John Thelwall, by his Widow* i (London, 1837), p. 367.
6. The Acts were 36 Geo. III, c. 7 & 8. The second was an 'Act for the more effectually preventing Seditious Meetings and Assemblies'. Clause XII was directed at Thelwall and enacted that any house, room, etc., where lectures, debates, etc., shall be held on 'any supposed public grievance, or any matters relating to the Laws, Constitution, Government, or Policy *of these kingdoms*', shall be deemed a disorderly house and punished accordingly. My italics for the words which gave to Thelwall a loophole for his Roman lectures.
7. He explained that he was giving a six months' adjournment to the lectures (after which time the period in which an action under the Two Acts could be taken would expire) in order to test the law: *The Tribune: A Periodical Publication, Consisting Chiefly of the Political*

Lectures of J. Thelwall, 3 vols. (London, 1795-6), iii, pp. 331-2.

8. *Courier*, 22 Aug. 1796.

9. John Thelwall, *An Appeal to Popular Opinion against Kidnapping and Murder including a Narrative of the Late Atrocious Proceedings at Yarmouth* (London, 1796), p. 13. See also Thelwall's letter, dated 8 July 1796, from Norwich, in *Moral and Political Magazine of the London Corresponding Society*, i (July 1796): 'the head and the heart – the understanding and the benevolence of the city are decidedly with us', including several persons of considerable property and 'many excellent citizens of both sexes ...with leisure and literary accomplishments'. For Norwich's intellectual Jacobinism, see C. B. Jewson, *Jacobin City* (Glasgow, 1975); Trevor Fawcett, 'Measuring the Provincial Enlightenment: The Case of Norwich', *Eighteenth Century Life*, new ser., viii, no. 1 (Oct. 1982).

10. Anne Plumptre to 'Dear Citizen' [George Dyer], n.d.: Norfolk Record Office, Norwich, MS. 4262. Anne is not to be confused with her more illustrious older sister, Annabella, also a staunch reformer.

11. Thelwall was in fact invited to Norwich by the talented author (and contributor to the *Cabinet*), Amelia Alderson, subsequently Opie: see Charles Cestre, *John Thelwall* (London, 1906), p. 128, n. 'A.A.' (presumably Amelia Alderson) also knew George Dyer and also addressed him as 'Dear Citizen': Emmanuel College, Cambridge, Archives, Col. 9. 13 (1), n.d. (but 1795?).

12. Henry Crabb Robinson to Thomas Robinson (his brother), 7 June 1796, and Thomas Amyot to H. C. Robinson, 16 Aug. 1796: Dr Williams's Library, London, Crabb Robinson correspondence. See also my 'Disenchantment or Default?', in C. C. O'Brien and W. D. Vanech (eds.), *Power and Consciousness* (London, 1969), p. 158. For Amyot, see the *Diary, Reminiscences and Correspondence of Henry Crabb Robinson*, ed. Thomas Sadler, 3rd edn, 2 vols. (London, 1872), i, p. 14.

13. Amyot to H. C. Robinson, 8 June 1796: Dr Williams's Lib., Crabb Robinson correspondence.

14. The Complete Works of William Hazlitt, ed. P. P. Howe, 21 vols. (London 1930-4), xii, *The Plain Speaker*, 'On the Difference between Writing and Speaking', p. 264.

15. *Moral and Political Magazine of the London Corresponding Society*, i (Oct. 1796), reporting Thelwall's lecture on the Two Bills, 9 November 1795.

16. *Diary, Reminiscences and Correspondence of Henry Crabb Robinson*, ed. Sadler, i, p. 176 (28 July 1811).

17. A long report on the election in *Moral and Political Magazine of the*

London Corresponding Society, i (July 1796), signed 'R.D.' [R. Dinmore?]. For Anne Plumptre, see n. 10 above. Thelwall has a sharp comment on Gurney's lukewarm candidature in *The Rights of Nature* (London, 1796), i, p. 26.

18. A Lover of Order' [William Godwin], *Considerations on Lord Grenville's and Mr. Pitt's Bills* (London, 1795). The incident is discussed in Cestre, *John Thelwall*, pp. 134-40, and his Appendix, pp. 201-4.

19. *Tribune*, ii (1796), preface, p. xvii; and iii, no. 38 (1796), pp. 101.5.

20. Amyot to H. C. Robinson, 16 Aug. 1796 (see n. 12 above). In fact Godwin continued to keep his distance from Thelwall (and from all activists). William Taylor was a leading authority on and translator of German literature.

21. T. J. Mathias, *The Pursuits of Literature*, 9th edn (London, 1799), p. 355. In a footnote Thelwall is described as an 'indefatigable incendiary' (p. 356).

22. In Public Record Office, London (hereafter P.R.O.), K.B. 1/29, and in Thelwall, *Appeal to Popular Opinion*. I have drawn upon both sources in my account.

23. Subsequently twenty-two persons subscribed £50 each to prosecute the offenders. Those swearing depositions included four merchants, one gentleman, one carpenter, one single woman, one fiddler (and his son), one carter, one shipwright, one coachman, one book-keeper, one brewer. I have not established what was the outcome of the case, except that Thelwall recalled many years later that Captain Roberts, the ring-leader, was promoted to the command of a 74-gun ship and sent to the West Indies 'to be out of the way of justice'. See depositions in P.R.O., K.B. 1/29; Thelwall, *Appeal to Popular Opinion, passim; Selections from the Papers of the London Corresponding Society*, ed. Mary Thale (Cambridge, 1983), p. 365; [Cecil Thelwall], *Life of John Thelwall*, i, p. 436.

24. From the account in the *Courier*, 22 August 1796 (perhaps by Thelwall?) reprinted in Thelwall, *Appeal to Popular Opinion*.

25. The books included 'Roman Antiquities of Dionysius of Halicarnassus', Plutarch's Lives and Walter Moyle's Treatise on 'the Lacedemonian Government': Thelwall, *Appeal to Popular Opinion*, p. 25. Thelwall also drew heavily on Moyle's *An Essay upon the Constitution of the Roman Government*, which he republished with commentary as *Democracy Vindicated* (Norwich, 1796): see Hampsher-Monk, 'John Thelwall and the Eighteenth-Century Radical Response to Political Economy', pp. 2, 16.

26. See Linda Colley, *Britons: Forging the Nation*, 1707-1837 (New Haven, 1992), esp. ch. 5. I do not mean to challenge Linda Colley's persuasive analysis, but only to suggest that we should also remember whom loyalism was exercised against. Thelwall commented sharply that ' "God save the king" ...has been made the war-hoop of tumult and civil commotion': Thelwall, *Appeal to Popular Opinion*, p. 48.

27. There was a rumour, which Thelwall believed, that he was to be put on a Russian ship and taken to Siberia!

28. Thelwall's reminiscence in the *Champion*, 25 October 1819. Windham was reported as declaring in the Commons (23 November 1795) that ministers 'were prepared to exert a vigour more than the laws': Anon., *The History of the Two Acts* (London, 1796), p. 386.

29. Others were William Frend and George Dyer. John Thelwall, writing to Thomas Hardy from Yarmouth, 24 August 1796, sent warm messages of solidarity 'to Friend in particular, & to that Walking Benevolence George Dyer': see Appendix.

30. *Anti-Jacobin*, no. 17, 5 Mar. 1798, p. 135, 'The New Coalition'.

31. The *Independent Whig* perhaps saw the *Champion* as a competitor, and attacked Thelwall repeatedly: 22 November 1818, 21 February, 13 and 27 June 1819.

32. *Champion*, 6 June 1819.

33. Slightly different accounts are given *ibid.* and in the 'Prefatory Memoir' to John Thelwall, *Poems Chiefly Written in Retirement* (Hereford, 1801), p. xxx (hereafter Thelwall, 'Prefatory Memoir'.).

34. Annual Register, 1797, 'Chronicle', pp. 15-16. Dr Peter Crompton (see n. 90 below) wrote to Thelwall, 11 September 1800, reminding him of the chapel 'where I and many others were almost knocked on the head': Pierpont Morgan Library, New York, MA 77 (19).

35. *Champion*, 25 Oct. 1819. The friend is identified as James Moorhouse, an 'old Jack' who remained an active reformer in Stockport until post-war years, when he was indicted for his part in the Peterloo meeting.

36. Goodwin, *Friends of Liberty*, p. 414; Jewson, Jacobin City, pp. 81-2; *Address from the Patriotic Society of that City* (Norwich, 1797; copy in Seligman Collection, Columbia University, New York).

37. According to Charles James Fox, during riots a straw effigy of Priestley was carried through the streets, enclosing the heart of an animal, which, when pierced with a pike, made the effigy stream with blood. The effigy was then burned and the heart was eaten! *History of the Two Acts*, p. 422.

38. See 'Rough Music', in my *Customs in Common* (London, 1991).

39. *History of the Two Acts*, p. 421.
40. Among hunts founded in these loyal years were the Atherstone (1804), Berkeley (reorganized 1807), Bicester (1800), Carmarthenshire, Cattistock, Cheshire (1802), Craven, Eggesford (c. 1798), Captain Johnstone's (1808), Ledbury, New Forest hunt club, Newmarket and Thurlow (1793), Oakly (1800), Puckeridge (c. 1799), S. Staffs, Surrey Union (1799), Wheatland, Worcester: *Bailey's Fox-Hunting Directory, 1897-8* (London, 1897).
41. Thelwall, 'Prefatory Memoir', p. xxx.
42. *Ibid.*, pp. xxx-xxxii; Goodwin, *Friends of Liberty*, pp. 405-6; Cestre, *John Thelwall*, pp. 125-7.
43. The naval mutiny at Spithead was then in progress.
44. A jocular reference to his imprisonment in the Tower while awaiting trial for High Treason in 1794.
45. Thelwall to Thomas Hardy, Derby, 19 May 1797: see Appendix. For Thelwall's eulogy at Hardy's funeral in 1832, see [Cecil Thelwall], *Life of John Thelwall*, i, pp. 430-6.
46. In December 1797 Thelwall sent a letter to the committee of the London Corresponding Society in which he loftily reproved members for wrangling, and suggested that instead they should spend their time 'in reading and political discussion': he sent twelve copies of his own *The Rights of Nature* and proposed that twelve men should be appointed to read the book to divisions: *Selections from the Papers of the London Corresponding Society*, ed. Thale, p. 377, n.
47. *Monthly Magazine*, Aug. 1799, p. 532. Long extracts from his journal of 'A Pedestrian Excursion through Several Parts of England and Wales' appeared in successive numbers of the *Monthly Magazine*, but, alas, these were discontinued before he reached Somerset. A fuller version of the journal once existed and it was drawn upon by Cestre: see Appendix.
48. Coleridge's end of the correspondence, which commenced in April 1796 is to be found in the *Collected Letters of Samuel Taylor Coleridge*, ed. E. L. Griggs, 6 vols. (Oxford, 1956-71), i. Only one letter of Thelwall's to Coleridge seems to have survived, in British Library, London, Poole Papers, Add. MSS. 35,344; see also Warren E. Gibbs, 'An Unpublished Letter from John Thelwall to S. T. Coleridge', *Mod. Lang. Rev.*, xxv (1930), pp. 85-90.
49. *Tribune*, ii, no. 16 (1796), pp. 16-17.
50. *Monthly Magazine*, Sept. 1799, p. 619. The magazine's extracts continued in November 1799, January, February and April 1800, and concluded at Stonehenge.

51. See esp. *John Thelwall: Political Writings*, ed. Claeys.

52. Thelwall to J. Wimpory, 15 Feb. 1797: Houghton Library, Harvard University, fms Eng. 957.2 (19). Cf. Coleridge to Thelwall, 9 Feb. 1797, in *Collected Letters of Samuel Taylor Coleridge*, ed. Griggs, i, no. 176, pp. 306-8.

53. John to Stella Thelwall, 'All fox den', 18 July 1797: Pierpont Morgan Lib., MA 77 (17). See also J. Dykes Campbell, *Samuel Taylor Coleridge* (London, 1894), p. 73.

54. *Monthly Magazine*, Sept. 1799, p. 618. His companion was J. Wimpory, a shoemaker of Gosport, Hants, who had to leave him at Bath.

55. The best account is in Nicholas Roe, *Wordsworth and Coleridge: The Radical Years* (Oxford, 1988), pp. 234-62, which places the spy episode in context. See also the same author's excellent 'Coleridge and John Thelwall: The Road to Nether Stowey', in Richard Gravil and Molly Lefebure (eds.), *The Coleridge Connection* (Basingstoke, 1990), pp. 60-80. These replace the earlier account in A. J. Eaglestone, 'Wordsworth, Coleridge, and the Spy', in E. Blunden and E. L. Griggs (eds.), *Coleridge Studies by Several Hands* (London, 1934), pp. 73-87. Briefer accounts are in Mrs Henry Sandford, *Thomas Poole and his Friends*, 2 vols. (London, 1888), i, pp. 232-44; Mary Moorman, *William Wordsworth: A Biography*, 2 vols. (Oxford, 1957-65), i, pp. 329-33; Stephen Gill, *William Wordsworth: A Life* (Oxford, 1989), pp. 126-8.

56. J. Vellum had been thrown out of his farming tenancy in Rutland, and Thelwall said he had been driven out by a Lord of the Bedchamber [Lord Winchelsea?] because of his 'Jacobinical' associations: Thelwall, 'Prefatory Memoir', p. xxxvi; [Cecil Thelwall], *Life of John Thelwall*, i, p. 144, n.

57. John to Stella Thelwall, 18 July 1797 (see n. 53 above).

58. The Collected Works of Samuel Taylor Coleridge, 16 vols. (Bollingen ser., lxxv, Princeton, 1969-), xiv, *Table Talk*, ed. Carl Woodring, 2 vols., i, 24 July 1830, pp. 180-1, and n. 6. The incident impressed all three men, and each left a different account of it. In Wordsworth's anodyne recollection, Coleridge said: 'This is a place to reconcile one to all the jarrings and conflicts of the wide world'. 'Nay', said Thelwall, 'to make one forget them altogether'. See Christopher Wordsworth, *Memoirs of William Wordsworth*, 2 vols. (London, 1851), i, p. 105; *The Poetical Works of William Wordsworth*, ed. E. de Selincourt and Helen Darbishire, 5 vols. (Oxford, 1940-49), i, p. 363, Fenwick note to 'Anecdote for Fathers'. John Thelwall's account is

fictional: in his novel *The Daughter of Adoption*, 4 vols. (London, 1801), i, p. 283, the beautiful dell is set in St Domingo, where 'Henry' says, bantering, 'What a scene, and what an hour ...to hatch treason in'. 'What a scene, and what an hour', replied Edmund, with most undisturbed composure, 'to make one forget that treason was ever necessary in the world!'.

59. *Poetical Works of William Wordsworth*, ed. de Selincourt and Darbishire, i, p. 363, Fenwick note to 'Anecdote for Fathers'.

60. Coleridge to Josiah Wade, 1 Aug. 1797, in *Collected Letters of Samuel Taylor Coleridge*, ed. Griggs, i, no. 200, p. 339. But Coleridge added that Thelwall was 'the only *acting* Democrat, that is honest'.

61. J. Walsh to John King, Stowey, 16 Aug. 1797: P.R.O., H.O. 42/41: 'It is reported here that Thelwall is to return soon to this Place and that he is to occupy a part of Alfoxton House'.

62. Coleridge to Thelwall, 21 Aug. 1797, in *Collected Letters of Samuel Taylor Coleridge*, ed. Griggs, i, no. 204, p. 343.

63. Roe, *Wordsworth and Coleridge*, p. 258; Sandford, *Thomas Poole and his Friends*, i, p. 235. Coleridge suggested to Thelwall that he might come back in a few weeks, take lodgings in Bridgwater, and familiarize the people with 'the *monstrosity* of the thing'.

64. Lines, Written at Bridgewater, in Somersetshire, on the 27th of July, 1797; during a Long Excursion, in Quest of a Peaceful Retreat', in Thelwall, *Poems Chiefly Written in Retirement*, pp. 126-32. Other passages from this poem are cited in my *The Making of the English Working Class* (Penguin edn, Harmondsworth, 1970), pp. 180-1, and 'Disenchantment or Default?', pp. 160-1.

65. *Anti-Jacobin*, no. 36, 9 July 1798, p. 286. Thelwall probably already knew Southey, and he knew Lamb, who preceded him at Stowey by a week: see Winifred F. Courtney, *Young Charles Lamb*, 1775-1802 (London, 1982), pp. 144-6.

66. Portland to the Mayor of Bristol, 7 Aug. 1797: P.R.O., H.O. 43/9.

67. On Leaving the Bottoms of Glocestershire', in Thelwall, *Poems Chiefly Written in Retirement*, p. 139. The families are named as Norton, Newcomb and Partridge. Cestre quotes several passages from Gloucestershire and Wales in the 'Pedestrian Excursion' (the MS. then in his hands: see Appendix) – these mainly concern wages and conditions and the manufacturing system.

68. Complete Works of William Hazlitt, ed. Howe, viii, *Table-Talk*, 'On Genius and Common Sense', p. 34. Hazlitt uses the anecdote to illustrate the unconscious association of ideas.

69. John Taylor was a journalist who wrote for the *Anti-Jacobin*, and who

had at times served as informer, especially in 1794, when he put in more than sixty reports, many on Thelwall's lectures: see Emily Lorraine de Montluzin, *The Anti-Jacobins, 1798-1800* (Basingstoke, 1988), pp. 151-4; Clive Emsley, 'The Home Office and its Sources of Information and Investigation, 1791-1801', *Eng. Hist. Rev.*, xciv (1979); *Selections from the Papers of the London Corresponding Society*, ed. Thale, passim.

70. There is an admirable study by P. J. Corfield and Chris Evans, 'John Thelwall in Wales: New Documentary Evidence', *Bull. Inst. Hist. Research*, lix (1986), pp. 231-9. This should be read beside my own account, which as far as possible does not repeat it but draws on new material.

71. Thelwall to Thomas Hardy, Derby, 25 Oct. 1797: see Appendix.

72. Diary, Reminiscences and Correspondence of Henry Crabb Robinson, ed. Sadler, i, p. 15. 'Stella' was in fact Susan Vellum.

73. Thelwall to Thomas Hardy, Derby, 25 Oct. 1797: see Appendix.

74. Thelwall to Thomas Hardy, 16 Jan. 1798, in Corfield and Evans, 'John Thelwall in Wales: New Documentary Evidence', pp. 234-6.

75. Thelwall to Vellum (at Oakham), 10 Mar. 1794, in P.R.O., T.S. 11/951/3495.

76. See nn. 10-11 above. The first use of 'Yours fraternally' which I have noticed is in a letter to the 'Citizen Editor' of the *Moral and Political Magazine of the London Corresponding Society*, i (July 1796) from 'R.D.' of Norwich [R. Dinmore?'].

77. Thelwall's novel, *The Daughter of Adoption* – has much on the rational education of children, without punishments, bribes, etc.; see vol. i, pp. 58 ff.

78. Thelwall to Dr Peter Crompton, at Eton House, near Liverpool, 3 Mar. 1798, Houghton Lib., fms Eng. 947.2 (21).

79. Phillips was reported to draw £1500 receipts from each number of the magazine: J. E. Cookson, *The Friends of Peace* (Cambridge, 1982), p. 90. For Dr John Aikin, the brother of Mrs Barbauld, see ibid., pp. 99-100. See also G. Carnall, 'The *Monthly Magazine*', *Rev. Eng. Studies*, new ser., v (1954).

80. *Monthly Magazine*, May 1798, pp. 343-6; July 1798, pp. 20-21. There were also several contributions signed with three stars (H H H) which, on internal evidence, are Thelwall's: *ibid.*, 1798, pp. 177-9; June 1798, pp. 418-21; Dec. 1798, p. 409.

81. See Nicholas Roe, *The Politics of Nature* (Basingstoke, 1992), ch. 6, 'The Politics of the Wye Valley'. See also Richard Warner, *A Walk through Wales* (Bath, 1798).

82. H. C. Robinson to J. T. Rutt, 28 Oct. 1799: in Dr Williams's Lib., Crabb Robinson correspondence; also to his brother, Thomas Robinson, 21 Oct. 1799.

83. More than one informer reported to the Home Office as to Thelwall's extensive correspondence; thus R. Gwynne – 'he constantly writes and receives from twelve to twenty letters daily', and E. Edwards – 'a vast number of Letters by every Post': both April 1798, and cited in Corfield and Evans, 'John Thelwall in Wales: New Documentary Evidence', p. 236.

84. Thelwall thanked Crompton for a donation of £15 (a large sum indeed): Thelwall to Crompton, 3 Mar. 1798 (see n. 78 above). Hardy sent on £15 (which he had perhaps collected?): Thelwall to Thomas Hardy, 20 Sept. 1799: see Appendix.

85. William Rathbone, a wealthy Quaker (subsequently Unitarian), sent Thelwall £10: Thelwall to Crompton, 3 Mar. 1798 (see n. 78 above).

86. Revd W. Shepherd of Gateacre Baptist chapel, a fervent reformer, who many years later assisted Thelwall's widow in her memoir of her husband: see Appendix.

87. Presumably the Revd Joseph Smith.

88. Thelwall writes 'that poor worthy fellow Rushton', perhaps because this fervent abolitionist was blind?

89. On Roscoe and this whole circle, see Ian Sellers, 'William Roscoe, the Roscoe Circle, and Radical Politics in Liverpool, 1787-1807', *Trans. Hist. Soc. Lancs. & Cheshire*, cxx (1968), pp. 45-62; R. B. Rose, 'The 'Jacobins' of Liverpool, 1789-1793', *Liverpool Bull.* (Libraries, Museums & Arts Committee), ix (1960-1).

90. Crompton was a medical doctor and brewer, who moved from Derby to Liverpool (Eton House, Wavertree) in 1798. He stood as parliamentary candidate for Nottingham in 1796 and again in 1807.

91. See Corfield and Evans, 'John Thelwall in Wales: New Documentary Evidence', p. 238, n. 62. There is a fragment of a letter from Thelwall to Joseph Strutt, n.d., in which he writes: 'The Storm is past but I do not forget the Mast I clung to in the hour of wreck': Birmingham City Reference Library (Archives), Galton MSS. 507.

92. There is no definite evidence that Thelwall knew either of the Wedgwood brothers, but it is possible. Their interest in supporting literary radicals is testified by their handsome annuity to Coleridge in 1798, and the Wedgwood pottery issued a coffee service in the same year which showed Britannia between two female figures, one with an olive branch, the other with a cap of liberty.

93. A gentleman reported that Thelwall 'goes once a Fortnight to a Society

of Jacobins at the Crown and Sceptre in the City of Hereford': Corfield and Evans, 'John Thelwall in Wales: New Documentary Evidence', p. 236. These might have been surviving members of the dispersed Hereford Philanthropic Society: see *Selections from the Papers of the Corresponding Society*, ed. Thale, p. 364.

94.   This was argued of Thelwall by Gunther Lottes, *Politische Aufklärung und plebejische Publikum* (Vienna, 1979). See also H. T. Dickinson, *Liberty and Property* (London, 1979), p. 251.

95.   Ichabod Wright of Mapperley, near Nottingham, 17 July 1802: in P.R.O., H.O. 42/65. Joseph Birch was a Whig merchant imported from Liverpool. See also M. I. Thomis, 'The Nottingham Election of 1802', *Trans. Thoroton Soc.*, lxv (1961), pp. 94-103.

96.   But there has recently been a welcome revision of this view: see John Dinwiddy, 'England', in Otto Dann and John Dinwiddy (eds.), *Nationalism in the Age of the French Revolution* (London, 1988), and Mark Philp (ed.), *The French Revolution and British Popular Politics* (Cambridge, 1991), editor's introduction and contributions of Dinwiddy and Roger Wells. Also, of course, Roger Wells, *Insurrection* (Gloucester, 1983) and *Wretched Faces* (Gloucester, 1988); and for ultra-Radical Grub Street 'Jacks', see Iain McCalman, *Radical Underworld* (Cambridge, 1988).

97.   Roe, *Wordsworth and Coleridge*, pp. 2-3, 263. The Swiss invasion occasioned Coleridge's poem of recantation, 'France: An Ode'.

98.   Thelwall to Thomas Hardy, 24 May 1798, transcribed in J. Holland Rose, *William Pitt and the Great War* (London, 1911), p. 352: see Appendix.

99.   Thelwall to 'Dear Bard', 10 May 1798: National Library of Wales, Aberystwyth, MS. 21283 E no. 471. My thanks to both David Jones and Chris Evans.

100. The visit took place between 4 and 10 August 1798: Mark L. Reed, *Wordsworth: The Chronology of the Early Years* (Cambridge, Mass., 1967), p. 245. Wordsworth told a correspondent that Coleridge 'proposed it to me one evening and we departed the next morning at six o'clock': Wordsworth to Henry Gardiner, 3 Oct. 1798 in *The Early Letters of William and Dorothy Wordsworth (1787-1805)*, ed. E. de Selincourt (Oxford, 1935), p. 201. Wordsworth commemorated the name of Llys Wen farm in his poem, 'Anecdote for Fathers'.

101. See Kenneth R. Johnston, 'The Politics of "Tintern Abbey" ', *Wordsworth Circle*, xiv, (1983); Roe, *Politics of Nature*, ch. 6.

102. Brecknockshire Quarter Sessions Book of Orders (1787-1815) (in county council offices), Midsummer 1798, p. 223. Thelwall,

gentleman, v. Roos Davies: 'The Defendant having pleaded guilty and the prosecutor inclining to be lenient', Davies was fined sixpence and bound over to keep the peace for two years.

103. Thelwall, 'Prefatory Memoir', pp. xxxvi-xxxvii.
104. *Ibid.*, p. xxxvii. Also p. xlviii, where he speaks of the 'fundamental point of morals' among the Welsh 'that nationality is to go before right'.
105. Mr Thelwall's Reply to the Calumnies, Misrepresentations, and Literary Forgeries, Contained in the Anonymous Observations on his Letter to the Editor of the Edinburgh Review (Glasgow, 1804), p. 26.
106. *Monthly Magazine*, 1 July 1800, p. 532.
107. Thelwall, 'Prefatory Memoir', p. xxxvii.
108. A Little Welch Farmer' Brecnocshire, in *Monthly Magazine*, Nov. 1798, pp. 323-4.
109. *Ibid., July 1800, pp. 529-34.*
110. *Ibid.*, p. 532.
111. Thelwall, 'Prefatory Memoir', p. xxxix. The draft of the warrant for a search for a 'packet of treasonable papers' on the Hereford wagon directed to Mr Thelwall, signed Portland, is in P.R.O., H.O. 42/46. Thelwall said that the packet included a letter of criticism from a literary friend, and another to Stella Thelwall from the friend's sister: Winifred Courtney has suggested to me that this could have been Charles and Mary Lamb. (The Wordsworths were then in Germany.)
112. Thelwall continued to work on it for many years, and he assured Crabb Robinson that he would win fame as an epic poet: *Diary, Reminiscences and Correspondence of Henry Crabb Robinson*, ed. Sadler, i, p. 37.
113. Sandford, *Thomas Poole and his Friends*, i, p. 234.
114. Thelwall to Thomas Hardy, 20 Sept. 1799: see Appendix.
115. *Monthly Magazine*, Feb. 1800, p. 94.
116. Thelwall, *Poems Chiefly Written in Retirement*, p. 147.
117. *Ibid.*, p. 159.
118. *Ibid.*, p. 145.
119. See Corfield and Evans, 'John Thelwall in Wales: New Documentary Evidence', pp. 237-8.
120. Thelwall, 'Prefatory Memoir', p. xlvi. Thelwall complained that the 'moral tendency of the Work' had been 'somewhat questioned'. In my view the work has no moral tendency and one cannot give any credit to Thelwall's statement that the ' abstract moral of the tale, is …That the purity of the sexual intercourse consists, exclusively, in the inviolable singleness of attachment …whatever be our theoretical opinion of the

ceremonial part of the institution, it is an absolute moral duty, in the present state of society, to conform with the established usage'. In other words Thelwall wished to ride both a Godwinian and a conventional horse. But the novel scarcely addresses the issue.

121. *Ibid.*, p. xxxviii.
122. *Ibid.*, p. xliii.
123. He relied on his old network of friends to support him. He asked Hardy to find him subscribers for his book of poems: Thelwall to Thomas Hardy, 28 Feb. 1801: see Appendix. And he wrote to George Dyer with a long list of books on antiquarian matters requested: Thelwall to George Dyer, Hereford, 12 Aug. 1801: New York Public Library, Carl H. Pforzheimer collection, Misc. 672.
124. Thelwall to Joseph Strutt, from Leeds, 20 Dec. 1801: Birmingham City Ref. Lib. (Archives), Galton MSS. 507/1. See also Corfield and Evans, 'John Thelwall in Wales: New Documentary Evidence', pp. 238-9.
125. The earliest notice I have found of Thelwall's elocution lectures is in Sheffield: *Leeds Mercury*, 14 Nov. 1801.
126. Thelwall, *Rights of Nature*, ii, p. 32. See also R. Dinmore (of Norwich), *An Exposition of the Principles of English Jacobins* (Norwich, 1797), and review in *Moral and Political Magazine of the London Corresponding Society*, ii, (Jan. 1797).
127. Burton R. Pollin, and Redmond Burke, 'John Thelwall's Marginalia in a Copy of Coleridge's *Biographia Literaria*', Bull. New York Public Lib., lxxiv (1970), p. 93.
128. Courtney, *Young Charles Lamb*, Appendix B, p 346.
129. Analytical Rev., Apr. 1798. Also *Anti-Jacobin Rev.*, Dec. 1798, pp. 687-9, which warmly approved of the portrait of 'Citizen Rant'.
130. Coleridge to Thelwall, 23 Jan. 1801, in *Collected Letters of Samuel Taylor Coleridge*, ed. Griggs, ii, no. 376. p. 668.
131. Coleridge to Thelwall, 23 Apr. 1801, *ibid.*, no. 395, pp. 723-4. Thelwall was then writing his 'Prefatory Memoir' to his new volume of *Poems*. A good account of the Coleridge-Thelwall relationship is in Roe, 'Coleridge and John Thelwall: The Road to Nether Stowey'.
132. John to Stella Thelwall, 29 Nov. 1803, Pierpont Morgan Lib., MA 77 (18).
133. Pollin and Burke, 'John Thelwall's Marginalia in a Copy of Coleridge's *Biographia Literaria*', p. 82. This was when Coleridge was writing in strong support of the second war.
134. *Ibid.* He notes that Coleridge 'talked to me at Keswick of his design of writing an elaborate demonstration of the truth of Christian revelation which should commence with a denial of the existence of god' (p. 88).

135. 'Stella' (Susan Vellum) died in 1816. Thelwall married again, Henrietta Cecil Boyle, in about 1819.

136. Cecil Thelwall to Wordsworth, 12 Nov. 1838: Dove Cottage Papers. Wordsworth replied, somewhat formally, that he 'retained towards Mr T. a very friendly feeling': *The Letters of William and Dorothy Wordsworth*, 2nd edn, vi, *The Later Years*, pt 3, *1835-1839*, revised and ed. Alan G. Hill (Oxford, 1982), pp. 639-41.

137. A Norwich reformer reported that Thelwall spoke 'from the Leads over Cozen's Shop. He is a most powerful speaker. I suppose between 4 and 5000 people heard every word distinctly': Jewson, *Jacobin City*, p. 62.

138. See Denyse Rockey, 'The Logopaedic Thought of John Thelwall, 1764-1834: First British Speech Therapist', *Brit. Jl Disorders of Communication*, xii, no. 2, (Oct. 1977); Denyse Rockey, 'John Thelwall, and the Origins of British Speech Therapy', *Medical Hist.*, xxiii (1979); Robin Thelwall, 'The Phonetic Theory of John Thelwall', in R. E. Asher and Eugénie J. A. Henderson (eds.), *Towards a History of Phonetics* (Edinburgh, 1981). Thelwall founded an institute for speech training in Liverpool in 1805, and soon moved it to London.

139. Thelwall to Thomas Hardy, from Manchester, 19 Mar. 1803: see Appendix.

140. Thelwall to Thomas Hardy, from Rochdale, 10 June 1803: see Appendix. Signed 'Yours, in civic and cordial fraternity'.

141. *Edinburgh Rev.*, Apr. 1803, pp. 197-202.

142. In fact any orchestration probably came from William Erskine, a friend of Walter Scott's.

143. John Thelwall, *A Letter to Francis Jeffray, Esq., on Certain Calumnies and Misrepresentations in the Edinburgh Review* (Edinburgh, 1804), p. 45.

144. Anon. [Francis Jeffrey], *Observations on Mr. Thelwall's Letter to the Editor of the Edinburgh Review* (Edinburgh, 1804), pp. 15-16.

145. Mr. Thelwall's Reply to the Calumnies, Misrepresentations, and Literary Forgeries, Contained in the Anonymous Observations on his Letter to the Editor of the Edinburgh Review.

146. Wordsworth to Thelwall, mid-Jan. 1804, in *The Letters of William and Dorothy Wordsworth*, 2nd edn, i, *The Early Years, 1787-1805*, revised and ed. Chester L. Shaver (Oxford, 1967), pp. 431-5. See also the editor's helpful notes on the whole issue, and also (on Jeffrey's side) Henry, Lord Cockburn, *Life of Lord Jeffrey*, 2nd edn, 2 vols. (Edinburgh, 1852), i, pp. 154-5.

147. Coleridge to Southey, 25 Jan. 1804, in *Collected Letters of Samuel Taylor Coleridge*, ed. Griggs, ii, no. 538, p. 1039.

148. Collected Works of Samuel Taylor Coleridge, iv, *The Friend*, ed. Barbara E. Rooke, 2 vols., ii, no 2 (8 June 1809), p. 25, n. But there is also in letters 10 and 11 (19 and 26 Oct. 1809), *ibid.*, pp. 134-149, an eloquent condemnation of anti-Jacobin witch-hunting.

149. *New Letters of Robert Southey*, ed. Kenneth Curry, 2 vols. (New York, 1965), i, p. 511.

150. Pollin and Burke, 'John Thelwall's Marginalia in a Copy of Coleridge's *Biographia Literaria*', pp. 81, 82, 93-4.

151. Marilyn Butler, *Romantics, Rebels and Reactionaries* (Oxford, 1981), ch. 6.

152. *Edinburgh Rev.*, Nov. 1814, p. 5.

153. *Ibid.*, p. 30.

154. Wordsworth, *Excursion*, ii. 235-62.

155. *Ibid.*, 266-72.

156. *Ibid.*, iii. 787-99.

157. *Poetical Works of William Wordsworth*, ed. de Selincourt and Darbishire, v, pp. 374-5.

158. George McLean Harper, *William Wordsworth*, 2 vols. (New York, 1960 edn), i, p. 189. See also M. Ray Adams, 'Joseph Fawcett and Wordsworth's Solitary', *P.M.L.A.* xlviii (1933); Roe, *Wordsworth and Coleridge*, pp. 23-7.

159. Complete Works of William Hazlitt, ed. Howe, iii, *The Life of Thomas Holcroft* (1810), p. 171, n. 1.

160. Thelwall, 'Prefatory Memoir', p. xxxviii.

161. Wordsworth, *Excursion*, ii. 293-314.

162. Thelwall to Crompton, 3 Mar. 1798, (see n. 78 above).

163. Wordsworth, *Excursion*, ii. 410-91.

164. *Ibid.*, iii. 50-66 ff.

165. *Ibid.*, 472-4.

166. He told Dr Crompton that 'if I could ever turn Christian again I should certainly be a Unitarian Quaker': Thelwall to Crompton, 3 Mar. 1798 (see n. 78 above). In the *Rights of Nature*, i, p. 26, he referred to the Quakers as 'that body of men, whom, of all religionists, I most revere and love'. He also (ibid., ii, p. 111) called a priest performing a marriage ceremony a 'conjuror in a black gown' muttering spells.

167. Thelwall appears to refer with some sympathy to theists in an anonymous contribution to the *Monthly Magazine*, 1 Sept. 1800, pp. 127-30.

168. Hazlitt reviewed the *Excursion* in several numbers of the Examiner: see *Complete Works of William Hazlitt*, ed. Howe, iv, p. 111. But Hazlitt also launched a more virulent assault on the narrowness of country

people than anything to be found in Jeffrey.

169. *Ibid.*, xix, *Literary and Political Criticism*, 'Character of Mr. Wordsworth's New Poem, The Excursion', p. 11.

170. See esp. Jonathan Wordsworth, *The Music of Humanit* (London, 1969).

171. Scholars now believe that the Solitary was first conceived and inserted into the gathering drafts of the *Excursion* in 1809: see Kenneth R. Johnston, 'Wordsworth's Reckless Recluse: The Solitary', *Wordsworth Circle*, ix (1978), pp. 131-144.

172. Wordsworth, *Prelude*, x. 370-81.

173. Wordsworth, *Excursion*, iv. 305-9.

174. Cf. Burke: 'in ability, in dexterity, in the distinctness of their views, the Jacobins are our superiors': cited in Thelwall, Rights of Nature, i, p. 47.

175. Thelwall to Hardy, from Liverpool, 12 Dec. 1805: see Appendix. Thelwall repeated some of these views in his annotations to *Biographia Literaria*: 'No enlightened friend of Liberty or of Man could wish success to the boundless ambition of Napoleon'. But he regretted also 'the little assistance I gave by my voice & pen to the hypocrites who pretending to war for the independence of nations sought to reduce all europe to abject subjection to the regal aristocracy of confederated legitimacy'. Pollin and Burke, 'John Thelwall's Marginalia in a Copy of Coleridge's Biographia Literaria', pp. 82, 83.

176. See *Diary, Reminiscences and Correspondence of Henry Crabb Robinson*, ed. Sadler, i, p. 248 (12 Feb. 1815): Thelwall 'talked of the "Excursion" as containing finer verses than there are in Milton'. It has been suggested that the supposed borrowings might have been from the themes and structure of Thelwall's long poem, *The Peripatetic* (1793), although this debt is now discounted. The borrowings could also have been from Thelwall's past situation, but would he have wished these to be acknowledged? Jonathan Wordsworth reports that Thelwall 'marked in the cadence of every line' in his copy of the Excursion but I have not seen this copy: introduction to Woodstock Books reprint of *Poems Chiefly Written in Retirement* (Oxford, 1989).

[Since these notes were written, material by Thelwall has been published in two volumes:

Claeys, Gregory (ed.), *John Thelwall: Political Writings* (University Park, Penn State Press, 1995)

Penelope Corfield and Chris Evans (eds.), *Youth and Revolution in the 1790s: Letters of William Pattison, Thomas Amyot and Henry Crabb Robinson* (London, Alan Sutton, 1996).]

APPENDIX

The problems of the survival, provenance and probable loss of
Thelwall manuscripts are complex. His widow, Cecil,
completed the first volume of a *Life* (1837), which concludes
with the passage of the Two Acts at the end of 1795. A second
volume was promised, 'containing an account of his domestic
history and of his labours in the field of literature, of the
Science of Elocution'. Cecil Thelwall clearly started work on
this volume but it never appeared. A letter survives from her to
the Revd W. Shepherd of Gateacre chapel, Liverpool, an old
acquaintance from Thelwall's 'Jacobin' days, who had agreed
to give her advice. In this she refers to 'a great variety of
manuscripts': the second volume would be 'entirely literary'
(Henrietta Cecil Thelwall to the Revd W. Shepherd, March
1835, Manchester College, Oxford, Shepherd Papers, vol. vii,
no. 79). What happened to those manuscripts is the problem.
Cecil died in 1863, and it seems that some of her papers
passed, perhaps by way of F. W. Cosens, to James Dykes
Campbell, a biographer of Coleridge. On his death these came
up at Sotheby's, where they were bought by Charles Cestre,
who was working on a thesis on the 'French Revolution and
the English Poets' (Cestre, *John Thelwall*, p. 15). Sotheby's
catalogue (June 1904) shows that these included his 'Notes of
a Pedestrian Excursion, Documents of Employment of Time in
Wales', MS (1799-1801), the *Fairy of the Lake*, MS.

autobiographical material relating to his imprisonment in the Tower, with five volumes of autograph letters, etc. (lots 344-5). In Cestre's text, which occasionally draws upon these, there are other indications: for example, (p. 195, n.) in one journal there was 'a large number of names of artisans, shopkeepers, dissenting ministers, schoolmasters, by whom he was entertained during his tour through the provinces ...'

All this material would be most valuable, in providing a profile of Jacobinism in the later 1790s. But there is reason to fear that it is now lost. Both David Erdman (then of the New York Public Library) and I approached Professor Cestre independently to ask what had happened to the collection. To Erdman he replied, in May 1954, 'unfortunately I lent or sold the Thelwall MSS I don't remember to whom (it was 50 years ago). I am sorry I cannot help you'. To me he gave a different account, some three years later: 'Unfortunately my library was very much damaged and plundered by the German occupants during the war. My Thelwall books have disappeared' (24 September 1957). Subsequent enquiries in Paris turned up nothing. There is a dwindling chance that the collection may survive somewhere.

Thelwall was a prolific correspondent, notably in his Llys Wen years, and a few letters survive in British and American libraries, as the footnotes to my article indicate. There is a puzzle surrounding his letters to Thomas Hardy. It is not clear when and why these letters were detached from Hardy's papers, some of which survive in the British Library, Place Papers. In any case, thirteen of these letters evidently survived, and at some time after the Second World War eight of these were bought by the poet, Edgell Rickword. It is clear from the numeration on the letters that five of the original series were missing: no. 1, at some date before August 1796; no. 6, at a date between 25 October 1797 and 20 September 1799; and nos. 8, 9 and 10, at dates between 20 September 1799 and 19

March 1803. Rickword sold his letters on (presumably through the trade), but before doing so he made a transcript of all of them except no. 12, 10 June 1803, which he noted as 'entirely given up to personal financial tangles'. He also published extracts from the letters in the *Times Literary Supplement* ('Thelwall to Hardy: From a Correspondent', 19 June 1953, p. 402), where they have been little noticed. Edgell Rickword kindly sent to me a copy of his transcripts, which I have used in preparing this article.

Of the missing letters there has been no sign of no.1; no.6 (dated Hereford, 16 January 1798) turned up unexpectedly in the Dunedin Public Library, New Zealand, (Reed Rare Books Collection), and has been edited by P. J. Corfield and Chris Evans, in 'John Thelwall in Wales: New Documentary Evidence', *Bulletin of the Institute of Historical Research*, vol. lix, no. 140, November 1986; another letter (which might equally be no. 6) dated 24 May 1798 is in part transcribed in J. Holland Rose, *Life of William Pitt* (1923), vol. ii, p. 352, where the source is given as Mr A. M. Broadley's MSS,; and there is a hint of another (presumably no. 8, 9 or 10) in Catalogue 971 (1973) of Francis Edwards Ltd, where it is described as one page, sm. quarto, dated Hereford 28 February 1801, and concerned with drumming up subscribers for his *Poems*. I must thank Penelope Corfield for her great help in sorting this mystery out. It is probable that more Thelwall manuscripts are scattered in libraries across three continents, and this appendix may help to bring some to light.

NOTES ON SOURCES

EDUCATION AND EXPERIENCE
This lecture was given in Leeds in 1968 as the fifth annual Albert Mansbridge Memorial Lecture. It is included as an introduction to the essays on the English Romantics as it illustrates Edward's use of the concept of 'experience' in history, literature and education.

DISENCHANTMENT OR DEFAULT? A Lay Sermon
This was originally given as one of the Albert Schweitzer lectures series at New York University in 1968. It was first published in O'Brien and Vaneck (eds.) *Power and Consciousness*, NYU Press, New York, 1969.

WORDSWORTH'S CRISIS
First published in *London Review of Books*, 8 December 1988.

BENEVOLENT MR GODWIN
First published in *London Review of Books*, 8 July 1993.

SAMUEL TAYLOR COLERIDGE The Poet and his Editors
The three essays that make up this section were written between 1971 and 1979 as reviews of successive volumes of

the Collected Works of Coleridge. Some of the material would have formed part of an extended study of Coleridge which was never completed.

BLISS WAS IT IN THAT DAWN The Matter of Coleridge's Revolutionary Youth

First published in the *Times Literary Supplement*, 6 August 1971, reviewing: James Dyke Campbell, *Samuel Taylor Coleridge*, Lime Tree Bower Press, 1971; *The Collected Works of Samuel Taylor Coleridge*, Vol 2: *The Watchman*, edited by Lewis Patton; Vol 3: *Lectures 1795: On Politics and Religion*, edited by Lewis Patton and Peter Mann, Routledge and Kegan Paul, 1971; Frida Knight, *University Rebel*, Gollancz, 1971.

THE LIGHT AND THE DARK

Times Literary Supplement, 24 May 1974. *The Notebooks of Samuel Taylor Coleridge*, edited by Kathleen Coburn, Vol 3, 1808-1819, Routledge and Kegan Paul, 1974.

A COMPENDIUM OF CLICHÉ
THE POET AS ESSAYIST

The Wordsworth Circle, Vol X, no 3, (Summer 1979). *The Collected Works of Samuel Taylor Coleridge; Essays on his Times*, edited by David V. Erdman. 3 volumes, Princeton University Press, 1978.

HUNTING THE JACOBIN FOX

When I commenced this research many years ago I was given most generous help by David Erdman. More recently I have received help and advice from Greg Claeys, Penelope Corfield, James Epstein, Nicholas Roe and Dorothy Thompson.

AFTERWORD

One lecture which Edward gave more than once when he taught the subject of the seventeen nineties was on the 'woman question' in the decade. The figure who has been taken to embody this aspect of early romanticism was Mary Wollstonecraft, whose life and work he had studied and on whom he intended to write more fully. The one short piece which he wrote about her has already been republished in an earlier collection and is one of his best short pieces.* He intended, however, to place her in the context of a wider movement for change than has usually been recognised, and also to look at the effect on ideas about equality between the sexes of the counter-revolution in thought and behaviour which followed on from the Terror. His notes on the subject are not sufficiently complete or ordered to reconstruct a full account which would do justice to the ideas which he set out in its tentative introduction. His proposed title was 'The defeat of the rights of woman', and he began by saying:

---

*   *Mary Wollstonecraft* originally published in *New Society*, 19 September 1974, reprinted chapter one in *Persons and Polemics* (Merlin Press, 1994).

223

THE ROMANTICS

This will be a dismal lecture. And also not a very well prepared one. For some years I have been keeping files on the rights of women in the 1790s; and also on the defeat. It is now becoming two files: but the first remains slim, the second enlarges with each year.

This is not, I am convinced, a true representation of the position. Something large was happening in feminine sensibility among the middle classes in the 1790s – perhaps even beginning to happen between men and women. But scarcely had this small wave begun to rise and crest than it was overtaken by the far deeper wave of counter-revolution. It was the counter-revolution which swept on into the nineteenth century and carried as far as Victorianism. All that then remained of the movement in the 1790s was the vexed and controversial memory of one, Mary Wollenstonecraft.

I don't in any way wish to belittle Wollstonecraft. I'll return to her. But excessive attention to her and – rather less – to a few women writers, Mary Hayes, Mrs Robinson, Mrs Barbauld has been at the expense of a more thorough investigation of the wider shifts in sensibility in the 1790s.

But this investigation is difficult. it involved attention to literary mediocrities – correspondence columns of journals – private diaries and correspondence – a critical use of novels etc. If there were (indeed) hundreds or thousands of little Mary Wollstonecrafts between about 1792 and 1798 it is difficult to find them [Anne R, Mary Hays, Amelia Alderson, Priscilla Wakefield, Ann Plumtre] I haven't found them, but perhaps can suggest some places and ways in which they might be found.

There was of course already before the French Revolution and Mary Wollstonecraft a strong and enlightened tradition in certain quarters of Dissent – chiefly among Unitarians and Quakers. The letters of Mrs Clarkson or of Mrs Theophilus Lindsay show acute political, theological and intellectual independence and intelligence. Here serious education for girls was canvassed and practised: Mary Wollstonecraft herself came in close contact with this tradition in her school teaching days. Anne Seward and Mrs Barbould were among the writers...

At this point he would continue in his usual habit of lecturing without notes with illustrations from the pile of books and xeroxes of original sources which he always brought with him to the platform. It is not possible to reconstruct a clear narrative from the notes to the sources which follow this introduction, and indeed it is clear that he intended to do more work before he reached a point at which he was prepared to publish; it is however, of some importance to make clear that a study of this subject was to have been an integral part of the proposed volume.

D.T.